features

yOung
Exceptional
children

Monograph Series No. 5

Family-Based Practices

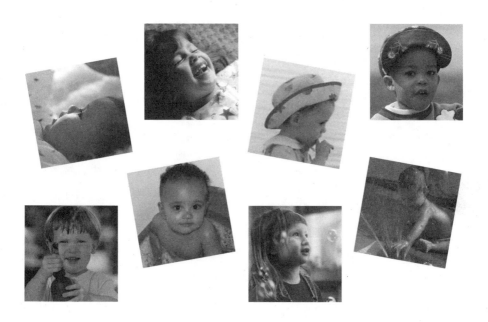

**THE DIVISION FOR EARLY CHILDHOOD
OF THE COUNCIL FOR EXCEPTIONAL CHILDREN**

Eva Horn, Michaelene M. Ostrosky, and Hazel Jones
Co-Editors

Disclaimer

The opinions and information contained in the articles in this publication are those of the authors of the respective articles and not necessarily those of the co-editors of *Young Exceptional Children (YEC) Monograph Series* or of the Division for Early Childhood. Accordingly, the Division for Early Childhood assumes no liability or risk that may be incurred as a consequence, directly or indirectly, of the use and application of any of the contents of this publication.

The DEC does not perform due diligence on advertisers, exhibitors, or their products or services, and cannot endorse or guarantee that their offerings are suitable or accurate.

Division for Early Childhood (DEC) Executive Board

President Laurie Dinnebeil
President Elect Beth Rous
Vice President Lynette Chandler
Past President Jennifer Kilgo
Secretary Barbara Wolfe
Treasurer Philip Printz
Governor Mark Innocenti
Members at Large Melissa Olive, Lynette Aytch, David Lindeman, Rosa Milagros Santos

DEC Standing Committee Chairs and Editors

Governmental Relations Committee Chair Diana J. LaRocco
Membership Committee Chair Sarintha Stricklin
Subdivision Committee Chair Diane Strangis
Personnel Preparation Committee Chair Mary Hendricks
Research Committee Chair Richard Roberts
Family Consortium Committee Chair Judy Swett
Multicultural Activities Committee Chair Lucinda Kramer
Publications Committee Chair Hazel Jones
Information Technology Committee Chair Nancy Fire
Student Activities Committee Chair Ilka Pfister
Editor, *Journal of Early Intervention* Pat Snyder
Editor, *Young Exceptional Children* Eva Horn
Executive Director Sarah Mulligan
Assisstant to the Executive Director Bethany Morris
Events Coordinator Betsy Dague
Governmental Relations Consultant Sharon Walsh

YEC Publications Committee

Chair, Hazel Jones, University of Florida
Carol Davis, University of Washington
Ann Garfinkle, Vanderbilt University
Eva Horn, University of Kansas
Robin McWilliams, Vanderbilt University Medical Center
Michaelene Ostrosky, University of Illinois at Urbana-Champaign
Ilene Schwartz, University of Washington
Barbara Smith, University of Colorado at Denver
Pat Snyder, University of New Orleans
Dale Walker, University of Kansas

Copyright 2004 by the Division for Early Childhood of the Council for Exceptional Children. All rights reserved. 07 06 05 04 03   6 5 4 3 2 1

No portion of this book may be reproduced by any means, electronic or otherwise, without the express written permission of the Division for Early Childhood.

ISSN 1096-2506 • ISBN 1-59318-069-1

Printed in the United States of America

Published and Distributed by:

SOPRIS
WEST
4093 Specialty Place • Longmont, CO 80504
(303) 651-2829 • FAX (303) 776-5934
www.sopriswest.com

634 Eddy Avenue • Missoula, MT 59812-6696
(406) 243-5898 • FAX (406) 243-4730
www.dec-sped.org

A Message From the Editors

Welcome to the fifth issue of the *Young Exceptional Children* Monograph Series. In this issue, we address the topic of family-based practices. The articles in this monograph highlight practices found in Chapter 4 (Trivette & Dunst, 2000) of *DEC Recommended Practices in Early Intervention/Early Childhood Special Education* (Sandall, McLean, & Smith, 2000).Trivette, Dunst, and the members of the recommended practice work group developed the following definition of family-based practices: *Family-based practices provide or mediate the provision of resources and supports necessary for families to have the time, energy, knowledge, and skills to provide their children learning opportunities and experiences that promote child development. Resources and supports provided as part of early intervention/early childhood special education (EI/ECSE) are done in a family-centered manner so family-based practices will have child, parent, and family strengthening and competency-enhancing consequences* (Trivette & Dunst, 2000, p. 39). DEC's recommended practices emphasize: (1) family and professionals practicing shared responsibility and collaboration; (2) practices, supports, and resources all working to strengthen family functioning; (3) individualization and flexibility as key characteristics of the practices; and (4) strengths- and assets-based practices at the foundation of our work. The implementation of family-based practices should provide families with a sense of confidence and competence about their children's learning and development.

The collection of articles in this monograph address the values, beliefs, and practices inherent in the recommended practices definition. They do so by describing specific strategies that will assist practitioners to collaborate with families in achieving the various components of the recommended practices. In addition, we provide a reprint of DEC's position paper on responsiveness to family cultures, values, and languages. You are encouraged to copy this statement and share it with your colleagues.

The collection of articles in this monograph address the values, beliefs, and practices inherent in the recommended practices definition.

The first article, by Gallagher, Fialka, Rhodes, and Arceneaux, lays a strong foundation for the importance of positive working relationships as the core of family-based practices. The authors challenge us to rethink the well-worn phrase "in denial." For professionals, they provide specific strategies for beginning this rethinking process, including supporting parents' hopes and dreams for their child, suspending judgment of families and their behavior, and being patient so that families can find their personal way through unexpected events. Wonderfully told personal stories, together with practical strategies, will have you "rethinking denial."

But how do we know if our helpgiving practices and interactions with families are family-centered? Wilson and Dunst provide practitioners and those who work with current or future practitioners with an evidence-based tool, the "Family-Centered Practices Checklist" (Family, Infant, and Preschool Program, 2002) to help answer this and other questions. They thoroughly describe the checklist, how it can be used to promote effective helpgiving practices, and give readers examples of completed checklists for several helpgiving contexts.

Barrera reminds us to pause and remember to honor differences. She reminds us that honoring the rich differences that are brought by children and families should be a fundamental practice in every program. We cannot wait until the appropriate resources are in place but must move forward to create resources so that honoring differences becomes a part of the ongoing process for each team member. Barrera, based on experiences and efforts of working with eight ECSE programs, describes how this can be done.

Flynn-Wilson and Wilson continue the theme of reminding us that families are composed of many different individuals as they ask, "What about fathers?" Fathers are in fact critical members of their children's teams and contribute in unique ways to children's development. In this article, Flynn-Wilson and Wilson provide clear examples of the father/child relationship and how service providers can seek fathers' input and active, ongoing involvement.

As families and professionals work together in partnership to develop an early intervention plan, they spend a great deal of time and thought in writing outcome statements to guide the course of service delivery. As Rosenkoetter and Squires tell us in their article, "The heart of the IFSP is the outcome statements, which define a planning team's shared vision for the child and its subsequent step-by-step plan for achieving that vision" (p. 51). This article provides readers with a clear process for developing meaningful outcomes and a tool for evaluating the outcomes generated. The ultimate goal is to ensure that families and professionals have generated outcomes with the greatest potential for positively impacting children's development.

To succeed in making an important impact, as described by the previous article, outcomes must progress from the framework of the IFSP to specific procedures for intervention. Jung and her colleagues describe strategies for taking this next step. In their article, a method for developing written intervention plans that can be used with families to assist in bridging the gap between the outcomes targeted on the IFSP and the interventions planned for implementation in natural environments is described. Specifically, Jung, Gomez, and Baird focus on refining the child-focused outcomes in IFSPs and developing plans to address these outcomes within the context of families' daily experiences.

As families and their children move from early intervention services and the IFSP to preschool early childhood special education services, new models of partnership and working together arise. The transition from a birth-to-three program to preschool can be stressful for families of young children with disabilities. In her article, Hadden uses a vignette to illustrate how this transition can be effectively facilitated when families and professionals work together. She includes examples of the roles that families may take in the process as well as ways that professionals can provide support for families' involvement.

In the final article, McCathren and Long describe a system for supporting home/preschool communication. Their notebook system is designed to help children remember what they did at school each day and provides caregivers with information that assists them to ask questions and talk with the children about their day. The notebook system includes strategies and experiences that have been found to support the development of language and literacy skills such as using predictable text, developing narrative skills by talking about daily events, and using pictures to support the meaning of text.

... [W]e hope that practitioners are inspired to reflect upon their practices with families and that families find support in their search for responsive services.

This fifth monograph concludes, as have the previous issues, with Catlett's "Resources Within Reason." Just as in each issue of *Young Exceptional Children*, Catlett has provided readers with low cost but high quality resource materials to support family-based practices.

As you read the articles in this monograph, we hope that practitioners are inspired to reflect upon their practices with families and that families find support in their search for responsive services. Collective behavior change will lead us toward our goal of families and professionals practicing shared responsibility and collaboration. Toward this end, the DEC board, together with the editors of this monograph, made a commitment to include family members as collaborators and decision makers for the monograph. Specifically, with assistance from the Family Consortium Committee, we included a family member as a reviewer for each article submitted for consideration. We extend our sincere thanks to Judy Swett, chair of the Family Consortium Committee, to each family member who participated, and to all the reviewers who contributed to this issue of the *Young Exceptional Children* Monograph Series.

Contributing Reviewers:

Harriet Able-Boone, University of North Carolina at Chapel Hill
Tomisina Adams, University of Florida
Dolores Appl, University of Maine at Farmington
Janet Bates, University of Kansas
Ann Bingham, University of Nevada-Reno
Patty Blasco, Portland State University
Eizabeth Borreca, University of St. Thomas, Houston, TX
William H. Brown, University of South Carolina
Joanna Burton, University of Illinois at Urbana-Champaign
Virginia Buysse, University of North Carolina at Chapel Hill
Lynette Chandler, Northern Illinois University
Kevin Cole, Washington Research Institute, Seattle, WA
Laurie Dinnebeil, University of Toledo
Sharon Doubet, University of Colorado at Denver
Alice Emery, University of Florida
Claudia Evans, Lawrence, KS
Paddy Favazza, University of Memphis
Kathleen Feeley, Long Island University, Southampton, NY
Lise Fox, University of South Florida
Ann Garfinkle, Vanderbilt University, Nashville, TN
Sandra Gautt, University of Kansas
Misty Goosen, University of Kansas
Sarah Hadden, University of Wisconsin-Eau Claire
Marci Hanson, San Francisco State University
Amy Harris-Solomon, Easter Seals Tennessee, Nashville, TN
Mary Louise Hemmeter, University of Illinois at Urbana-Champaign
Hannah Horst Schertz, Indiana University
Jennifer Hurley, Vanderbilt University, Nashville, TN
Ronda Jenson, University of Kansas
Gail Joseph, University of Colorado at Denver
Jean Kueker, Our Lady of the Lake University, San Antonio, TX
Cecile Komara, University of Kansas
Crystal Ladwig, University of Florida
Dave Lindeman, University of Kansas
Marisa Macy, University of Oregon
Chris Marvin, University of Nebraska
Susan Maude, Loras College, Dubuque, IA
Rebecca McCathren, University of Missouri
Mary McLean, University of Wisconsin-Milwaukee
Rosa Milagros Santos, University of Illinois at Urbana-Champaign
Linda Mitchell, Wichita State University
Melinda Morrison, Gainesville, FL
Chryso Mouzourou, University of Illinois at Urbana-Champaign
Leslie Munson, Portland State University
Jacqueline Murry, University of Illinois at Urbana-Champaign
Chelie Nelson, University of Kansas
Susan Palmer, University of Kansas
Carla Peterson, Iowa State University
Barb Phillips, Florida Atlantic University, Boca Raton, FL
Kristi Pretti-Frontczak, Kent State University, Kent, OH
Paige Pullen, University of Virginia

Megan Purcell, University of Kansas
Cheryl Rhodes, Georgia State University
Ilene Schwartz, University of Washington
Sean Smith, University of Kansas
Judy Swett, PACER Center, Inc., Bloomington, MN
Dawn Thomas, University of Illinois at Urbana-Champaign
Vickie Turbiville, Dripping Springs, TX
Rud Turnbull, University of Kansas
Laura Vagianos, LSUHSC Early Intervention Institute, New Orleans, LA
Dale Walker, University of Kansas
Robin Wells, University of Kansas
Mike Wischnowski, University of Rochester
Maria Wojtalewicz, University of Florida
Chien-Hui Yang, University of Kansas

References

Family, Infant, and Preschool Program. (2002). *Family-centered practices checklist.* Morganton, NC: Author.

Sandall, S., McLean, M., & Smith, B. J. (Eds.). (2000). *DEC recommended practices in early intervention/early childhood special education.* Longmont, CO: Sopris West.

Trivette, C., & Dunst, C. (2000). *Recommended practices in family-based practices.* In S. Sandall, M. McLean, & B. J. Smith (Eds.), *DEC recommended practices in early intervention/early childhood special education* (pp. 39-44). Longmont, CO: Sopris West.

Co-Editors: Eva Horn   Michaelene M. Ostrosky   Hazel Jones

evahorn@ku.edu   ostrosky@uiuc.edu   HAjones@coe.ufl.edu

Coming next!

The topic for the sixth YEC Monograph is
Interdisciplinary Teams. For more information,
check the "Announcements" section of
Young Exceptional Children (Volume 7, Number 1)
or go to **http://www.dec-sped.org**.

THE DIVISION FOR EARLY CHILDHOOD

DEC Position on Responsiveness to Family Cultures, Values, and Languages

Approved: April 2002

For optimal development and learning of all children, individuals who work with children must respect, value, and support the *cultures, values, and languages* of each home and promote the active participation of all families.[a] Legislation and recommended practices call for individualized approaches to serving infants, toddlers, and young children with special needs and their families. Individualized services begin with responsiveness to differences in race, ethnicity, culture, language, religion, education, income, family configuration, geographic location, ability, and other characteristics that contribute to human uniqueness.

Responsiveness grows from interpersonal relationships that reflect a mutual respect and appreciation for individuals' cultures, values, and languages. Responsiveness must be both personal and organizational for optimal outcomes of development and intervention services. Responsive early childhood programs and professionals honor the values and practices within the families being served as well as among the people providing the services.

Characteristics of responsive organizations include:

- Respect for the values and practices of all members;
- Encouragement of multiple viewpoints to enrich the whole organization;
- Seeking ways to extend competence of the leadership as well as practitioners, with regard to differences in family cultures, values, and languages;
- Development, implementation, and review of policies and procedures in recruitment and leadership development at all levels of service to ensure meaningful local, state, national, and international representation and participation of people from different cultural, ethnic, and language backgrounds;

- Encouragement and support of the development and dissemination of products that address family cultures, values, and languages; and

- Meetings and conference presentations that incorporate the impact of family cultures, values, and languages in all early childhood activities and services.

A definition of terms:

Culture refers to " ... shared and learned ideas and products of a society. It is the shared way of life of a people, including their beliefs, their technology, their values and norms, all of which are transmitted down through the generations by learning and observation" (Small, 1998, p. 72). *Values* refer to " ... emotionally laden beliefs about what is right or wrong, appropriate or inappropriate, desirable or offensive" (CLAS Early Childhood Research Institute, 1998, p. 9).

---

[a]The source of inspiration for this first sentence is *NAEYC's Position Statement on Responding to Linguistic and Cultural Diversity* (1995). Permission to copy not required. Distribution encouraged.

References

CLAS Early Childhood Research Institute. (1998). *CLAS Institute glossary.* Champaign, IL: University of Illinois at Urbana-Champaign.

Small, M. F. (1998). *Our babies, ourselves: How biology and culture shape the way we parent.* New York: Anchor Books.

Working With Families

Rethinking Denial

Peggy A. Gallagher, Ph.D., Georgia State University
Janice Fialka, MSW, Parent, Huntington Woods, MI
Cheryl Rhodes, MSW, Georgia State University
Cindy Arceneaux, Parent, Los Angeles, CA

Many years ago, Helen Keller's mother, Katie Keller, was insistent that the family not abandon the search to find the person who might be able to unlock the mystery of her daughter (Gibson, 1962). Despite the best advice and efforts of professionals and family, Mrs. Keller refused to have her daughter put in an asylum. Would Mrs. Keller be labeled "in denial" today? Well-meaning professionals might shake their heads at the IEP meeting and express their genuine concern that this mother is just not able to accept her daughter's pervasive disabilities. After all, it would be obvious to everyone that little Helen could not see or hear.

Wasn't Helen Keller's mother right to be optimistic about her daughter's potential? Mrs. Keller was acutely aware that Helen had serious and significant limitations. After all, she was helping to care for her child at home on a full-time basis. She knew through daily experiences that Helen was not like other children. However, Captain and Katie Keller had hopes and dreams for Helen and wanted her to have a chance to fulfill those dreams. Mrs. Keller wanted the professionals to have high expectations for her daughter even if she herself did not know how to reach her, and she persevered in her fight to obtain possibilities for Helen.

Even today, with research supporting well-planned and effective interventions, no one can accurately know or precisely predict what children with disabilities will accomplish and become in their future. Still, some professionals characterize parents as "in denial" when they think the parents do not accept their child's disabilities and limitations. It is important to explore the implications of the well-worn phrase "in denial," and to begin a discussion on reframing the concept of denial.

Stages and States of "In Denial"

Sands, Kozleski, and French (2000) reviewed the literature on the impact of children with disabilities on their families, and noted the focus on the distress of having a child with disabilities. They suggest that professionals may have developed a stereotypical view of these families as being under so much stress that the family cannot meet the challenges of daily life. Others have recognized that the presence of a child with a disability in a family can have many positive effects, and can even help to strengthen families (Turnbull & Turnbull, 2001).

The use of the term "in denial" in labeling parents of children with disabilities stems from Kubler-Ross' (1969) work on death and dying in which she outlines the stages of grief, concluding with the final stage of acceptance. Many professionals in social work, psychology, nursing, and education have been taught that these stages mirror the grief that parents experience due to the loss of their "perfect" child when they learn about their child's disability.

Howard, Williams, Port, and Lepper (1997) suggest that it may not be helpful for professionals to view family members as being in particular stages of grief. Family members process information in different ways and at different times. While the feelings expressed in Kubler-Ross' (1969) work are feelings parents may experience at given times, there are not necessarily stages of feelings that parents must pass through

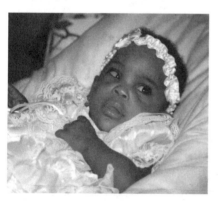

sequentially in order to reach the next stage. Some parents object to the rigidity of this model. In fact, parents report they sometimes experience feelings such as guilt, acceptance, despair, or denial all within a period of five minutes of dealing with their child with special needs. Kaster (2001) compares the feelings to a "roller coaster ride of emotions" (p. 186).

Miller (1994) likewise resists the concept of a linear stage model. She reports that parents do not feel that there are clearly delineated passages they must master before moving to the next stage. She instead refers to stages of adaptation to best describe the process the mothers she interviewed went through in adjusting to their children with disabilities. The four elements of adaptation she describes include surviving, searching, settling in, and separating. Miller (1994) views these stages as evolving not in a linear, developmental sequence, but rather having a circular, dynamic quality. She suggests that feelings come and go at expected and unexpected moments, some lingering, and some fleeting.

Several classic studies questioned the usefulness of a stage theory of adjustment to describe parental responses to their child with a disability. Featherstone (1980) suggested that some parents might not pass through the stages at all or might experience the stages in differing orders or at varying rates or intensities. Blacher (1984) conducted an extensive review of the existing literature and showed that families experience a wide range of responses to the diagnosis of their child's disability. She urged that further research document parents' feelings and responses. Winton, in 1990, reminded professionals to define "denial" as an internal coping strategy, which may be useful to some parents, rather than view the concept as a worrisome stage to be overcome before reaching the stage of acceptance.

Turnbull and Turnbull (2001) also urge professionals to look beyond the stages of grief. They suggest that feelings of denial and grief are emotions that may disappear and reappear in all families. These feelings often occur during transition periods for families who have children with disabilities, when the children move from one set of services to another. Thus, when a family has a child with a disability, the parents may have a range of emotional responses that all family members experience at various times (Sands, Kozleski, & French, 2000).

Different Perspectives

Miller (1994) views denial as a protective device used by a parent when he or she is not ready to deal with a problem or its implications. She suggests that parents sometimes choose to put off dealing with issues even when deep down they know something is wrong. Fialka (2001) notes that professionals may think of parents as being "in denial" when they seem withdrawn, hostile, or uninvolved. Harry (1997) proposed that professionals sometimes use the term "in denial" when actually the parent and professionals are in disagreement about the prognosis, diagnosis, program, or intervention strategy. Unfortunately, when this happens, the phrase "in denial" is sometimes applied in a judgmental way towards parents. In reality, each party simply possesses a different perspective and may not be sharing the same vision of the child and his or her future. When parents are judged solely from the professional's perspective, the professional may not genuinely listen to or engage parents in a conversation about their dreams and hopes for their child. If professionals categorize parents as "in denial," unaccepting, or difficult, professionals may lose the chance to understand and learn from the parents.

If professionals categorize parents as "in denial," unaccepting, or difficult, professionals may lose the chance to understand and learn from the parents.

Parents and professionals often enter into a working relationship with different expectations and perspectives. Such differences affect how each partner perceives the next step in intervention. For many professionals, a label, diagnosis, and/or prognosis can give direction and insight to their work with a child. They can consider which intervention techniques work best with children with that particular diagnosis. They know what they expect to happen with the child. During the initial diagnosis and during transition periods, parents may not appreciate the importance of a diagnosis or label. To parents, labels may be like foreign words creating chaos and a sense of inadequacy. Parents may question the meaning of the diagnosis, unsure about how it might affect the future of their child and family. They may feel unprepared for this new twist in life, and wonder how to assimilate so much information at once. Professionals should be cautious not to expect all parents to integrate new information about their child in the same manner or within the same time frame as the professional.

The professional's motivation for involvement in the field of early childhood special education may also innocently contribute to the chasm between perceptions held by parents and professionals. Many, if not most, professionals in special education typically enter into the work because they want to make a difference in the lives of children and families and make a contribution towards making the world better. During their training and education, they learn techniques, procedures, interventions, and theories that assist them in learning to help take care of people. This perspective is not wrong or harmful. Indeed, the desire to have a positive impact on others is noble and valuable. There are caveats, though, that accompany such a perspective. At times the desire to intervene—to do or to help—may have more relevancy to the professional than to the parent. Parents have many activities and challenges in their lives and may not always be able to find the time or energy to do what the therapist or teacher suggests (Fialka, 2000). When a parent does not seem to take advantage of the intervention ideas offered, professionals may be puzzled and wonder why the parent won't help the child. Professionals may feel frustrated and think that since they learned to teach children with special needs and have dedicated their professional life to doing so, the parents could at least cooperate. In such moments, professionals must seek out the support of a trusted colleague to vent their worries about the family (without breaking confidentiality, of course) and to think about other ways to support this family.

Understanding the Family Perspective

Many parents and professionals have heard or used phrases such as, "that parent is in denial," or "that father can't face the reality of his child's limitations," or "that mother refuses to admit that her child won't be able to ...." Sometimes when professionals use the phrase "in denial," the implied message is that the parents are not being realistic in their expectations of what their child can or will be able to do. Professionals should be careful not to judge a family when the family does not want to do things the way the professionals think is best.

Professionals should be cautious not to expect all parents to integrate new information about their child in the same manner or within the same time frame as the professional.

For instance, a father may say that his hope and goal for his three-year old daughter with severe cerebral palsy is for his daughter to walk. The professionals may think that this father is "in denial" and that he is totally unrealistic in thinking that this child will ever walk! Is the father "in denial"? Perhaps not. One possible scenario is that the father knows very well that the chances of his daughter walking are not very good. Yet if there is even the slightest chance that she might walk the father will continue to maintain that goal. Garnering all the support available to achieve this possible outcome, for his daughter to walk, is a reasonable path for this father to take.

Another possibility is that this father does understand and worries that his daughter may never be able to walk without some assistance. This thought may haunt him. His worry may be quietly and internally acknowledged, he may be able to whisper it in the privacy of his thoughts, but it may take more time and trust if he is ever to say it out loud to professionals. To formulate such worries into words is an enormous challenge, but to acknowledge them publicly to a stranger, including the caring professional, may be an unrealistic expectation for this father at this time.

A third possible meaning is that this father, upon initially hearing the new information about his daughter, is stunned and overwhelmed with unfamiliar thoughts such as the implications of not walking for his little girl and for his family. There is no easy place to rest such nagging thoughts. People need time to find their own personal way through unexpected news. Sometimes parents "put the pause button on" to attempt to slow down the speed of change. One mother in Idaho says that "Denial" is a place for her (Thurber, 1996). She asks that professionals not shake their heads and look down upon her when she wants to retreat from the hubbub of being a parent. "I know where I am and I need to be there sometimes. Then I come back to reality," she says.

People need time to find their own personal way through unexpected news. Sometimes parents "put the pause button on" to attempt to slow down the speed of change.

Suggestions for Professionals

Is there a better way to understand the family perspective when parents and professionals have different expectations for children with special needs? Recently, one of the authors asked her husband to explain his early impressions of their son with developmental disabilities who is now a teenager. During the first year of their son's life, she saw a child who was not progressing and appeared unable to accomplish most of the milestones of a typical one-year old. Her husband, on the other hand, remembered their son as a bit slower but basically doing okay. She asked her husband if, during those early years, he was "in denial." He paused and replied, "No, I wasn't in denial. I was in hope." He needed to be optimistic about his son's future. As delineated in Table 1, ways for professionals to rethink denial might include the following:

- *Support parents' hopes and dreams for their child.*
  Professionals can reframe "in denial" as the parents' way of being "in hope." They can help parents explore their dreams, hopes, and fears for their child. Professionals can encourage the parents' dedication to, determination, and high expectations for their child. This doesn't mean that professionals can't help the parents understand

Table 1: Shifting Your Perspective on Denial

Suggestions for professionals:

- Support parents' hopes and dreams for their child.

- Suspend judgment of families and their behavior.

- Be patient. People need time to find their own personal way through unexpected events.

- View this time as an opportunity to strengthen trust.

- Educate other professionals and family members to rethink denial.

and be realistic about their child and the disability. Professionals can support parents in their many roles as teacher, advocate, record keeper, and morale booster. Professionals can encourage parents to have hopes and dreams for their child. When parents and professionals work together as a team, the role of optimist can be a shared responsibility.

Parents can be the best advocates for and supporters of their children with special needs when they are armed with information, encouragement, and optimism. As one mother said, "Anna is 14 now but I still hope that she will change and be okay. I know that is not realistic and I'm not denying that she is severely disabled, but I still like to have hope. It helps me get through the day and night sometimes. Hope is my time to just dream." Professionals can help by giving parents information and encouragement.

Another mother explained, "Each small step today paves the way for future opportunities. The other day my 12-year old daughter spontaneously wrote the first two letters of her name for the first time. I watched with interest as she concentrated, saying the words her teachers and I have said to her over and over during practice. After eight years of hope, challenging therapists who wanted to eliminate prewriting skills from her IEP because she will never be a functional writer, I thought, 'you go girl.' The accomplishment buoyed me to face the next challenge."

Parents can be the best advocates for and supporters of their children with special needs when they are armed with information, encouragement, and optimism.

• *Suspend judgment of families and their behavior.*
Parents do not like to feel that professionals are intentionally or
unintentionally judging them. An example of the real difference
between denial and hope can be found in the story of a mother who
set aside college funds for each of her children, including her daughter with disabilities. While the mother was aware of the extent of
her young daughter's cognitive limitations and knew that her child's
test scores indicated that she would not likely ever be a candidate
for higher education, from the mother's perspective, the college
fund represented hope for the future. However, from the therapist's
perspective, this college fund was evidence of the mother's denial.
When questioned about her decision to have a college fund, the
mother exclaimed, "Well, maybe not, but I can always hope."

No one would suggest that the therapist withhold information
or not offer alternative ways of viewing the child's future. But to
focus on the college fund was to miss the essence of the real goal,
which is to support the child to reach her highest potential and
to support the parent to remain hopeful in order to continue to

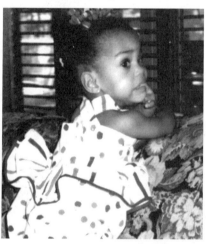

work with her child. It is important to examine the full range of
the actions and behaviors of the
parents before assuming that a
parent is in denial.

• *Be patient. People need time
to find their own personal way
through unexpected events.*
Sometimes parents attempt to
slow down the speed of change,
particularly when they are integrating new, and sometimes
painful and uninvited, information about their child. Learning
and understanding is a personal and private process that continues
over time. Professionals can help parents use time and optimism to
their advantage. Parents should not be made to think they have to
share everything or progress according to someone else's timetable!

• *View this time as an opportunity to strengthen trust.*
Some parents report that they find themselves distancing from professionals, thinking, "They are not going to understand." Others
may discount professional advice that does not consider their hopes

and dreams for their child. As a professional, take the opportunity to learn from each family and understand family differences. Families and individuals within families cope differently. The professional can carefully listen to understand the parent's perspective and can encourage the parent to talk about his or her concerns, doubts, and worries. Knowledge, acceptance, patience, and shared understanding increase trust.

- *Educate other professionals and family members to rethink denial.* The opportunities open to people with disabilities are expanding in ways that seemed unimaginable even a decade ago. People with disabilities, even severe disabilities, are living in their own homes, authoring books, attending colleges, holding jobs, starring in television shows, marrying, and having children. Not all people, whether or not they have a disability, will achieve the same dreams. The current vision is a hopeful one that invites a fuller participation for all people in a variety of dreams.

> ... [T]ake the opportunity to learn from each family and understand family differences. Families and individuals within families cope differently.

Over time, most parents rebuild their hopes and dreams for their child, learn to adapt to the circumstances in their lives, and remain steadfast in their concern for and commitment to their child with disabilities. The ways in which professionals understand and respect parents' efforts can significantly contribute to this process. Parenting a child with disabilities requires energy, determination, and perseverance. Perhaps hope provides the emotional fuel to persevere. We encourage professionals not to extinguish this hope by misrepresenting the parent's response as "in denial."

Professionals have the opportunity to educate others about the concept of denial. Talk to parents and other professionals and challenge them to think about how they are using the term. There can be another way to think about denial. Our hope is that through conversation and collaboration, parents and professionals will grow in their understanding of the many paths to acceptance and respect for the parents' own journey of rebuilding their dreams for their child.

Note
You can reach Peggy A. Gallagher by e-mail at spepag@langate.gsu.edu

References

Blacher, J. (1984). Sequential stages of parental adjustment to the birth of a child with handicaps: Fact or artifact? *Mental Retardation, 22,* 55-68.

Featherstone, H. (1980). *A difference in the family: Life with a disabled child.* New York: Basic Books.

Fialka, J. (2001). The dance of partnership: Why do my feet hurt? *Young Exceptional Children, 4*(2), 21-27.

Gibson, W. (1962). *The miracle worker.* New York: Bantam.

Harry, B. (1997). Leaning forward or bending over backwards: Cultural reciprocity in working with families. *Journal of Early Intervention, 21,* 62-72.

Howard, V. F., Williams, B. F., Port, P. D., & Lepper, C. (1997). *Very young children with special needs: A formative approach for the 21st century.* Upper Saddle River, NJ: Merrill.

Kaster, K. (2001). Different dreams. In S. Klein & K. Schieve (Eds.), *You will dream new dreams* (pp. 185-186). New York: Kensington.

Kubler-Ross, E. (1969). *On death and dying.* New York: Macmillan.

Miller, N. B. (1994). *Nobody's perfect: Living and growing with children who have special needs.* Baltimore: Paul H. Brookes.

Sands, D. J., Kozleski, E. B., & French, N. K. (2000). *Inclusive education for the twenty-first century.* Belmont, CA: Wadsworth/Thomson Learning.

Thurber, N. (1996). *A place called Denial.* Unpublished article.

Turnbull, A. P., & Turnbull, H. R., III (2001). *Families, professionals, and exceptionality: Collaborating for empowerment.* Upper Saddler River, NJ: Merrill.

Winton, P. J. (1990). Promoting a normalizing approach to families: Integrating theory with practice. *Topics in Early Childhood Special Education, 10,* 90-103.

Checking Out Family-Centered Helpgiving Practices

Linda L. Wilson, M.A., Family, Infant, and Preschool Program
Western Carolina Center, Morganton, NC

Carl J. Dunst, Ph.D., Family, Infant, and Preschool Program
Western Carolina Center, Morganton, NC, and
Orelena Hawks Puckett Institute, Asheville, NC

Charlie's mother, Irene, meets Martha at the door. Martha is an early childhood practitioner who is helping Irene identify resources for Charlie. Martha greets both Charlie and Irene and asks if this is still a good time to discuss the next steps in getting Charlie into child care. Irene says, "Yes," and invites Martha to sit with her on the sofa. Martha begins by asking Irene about the kind of child care center she wants for Charlie. Irene tells Martha that she would like a center that is warm and welcoming, open early, near the family's home, and relatively small. She prefers that Charlie be in a small center because she wants to protect him from illness and thinks he will get more attention from staff members because they will be caring for fewer children. Martha acknowledges these priorities and tells Irene about two neighborhood child care centers. Irene asks a few questions and Martha responds with what she knows. Martha tells Irene that one child care center seems friendlier than the other, and she suggests that Irene visit this center. Martha asks Irene what days and times would be good for her and tells her that she will call to arrange a visit that is convenient for Irene. Irene agrees and asks Martha to get back to her with confirmation of the visit.

How family-centered is this interaction? What is the likelihood that the parent will experience optimal positive benefits? What feedback should be provided to the practitioner about her helpgiving style? The evidence-based practice tool described in this article helps answer these and other questions about family-centered helpgiving practices. This article details the "Family-Centered Practices Checklist" (Family, Infant, and Preschool Program, 2002), including information on its development and application in promoting practitioners' use of evidence-based, family-centered helpgiving practices. First is a definition of family-centered helpgiving practices and a brief review of the research that provides the foundation for the Checklist items. Next is a description of the Checklist and how it is used to promote practitioners' adoption of effective helpgiving practices. Finally, examples of completed Checklists that have been used in work with families are presented.

Family-Centered Helpgiving Practices

In order for helpgiving practices to have optimal positive benefits, the ways in which a practitioner helps a family are as important as the help that is provided (Rappaport, 1981; Trivette & Dunst, 1998). A helpgiving relationship between a practitioner and a parent or caregiver is more likely to have optimal benefits when the parent sees himself or herself as an *agent of change* in achieving desired family-identified outcomes. Family-centered helpgiving is one way this can be accomplished.

Family-centered practices are those that treat families with dignity and respect; are individualized, flexible, and responsive to family concerns and priorities; include information sharing so that families can make informed decisions; honor family choice regarding any number of aspects of program practices and intervention options; use parent-professional collaboration and partnerships as a context for family-practitioner relations; and promote families' abilities to obtain and mobilize resources and supports necessary for them to care for and rear their children in competency-strengthening ways (Dunst, 1995; Shelton & Stepanak, 1994; Trivette & Dunst, 2000). Evidence indicates that when practices are family-centered in their orientation, or show a presumption toward family-centeredness, they have broader-based outcomes with respect to parent, family, and child benefits (see e.g., Davies, 1995; Dunst & Trivette, 1996 for reviews).

According to Dunst and Trivette (1996), family-centered practices have both *relational* and *participatory* components, and each component has two

> *A helpgiving relationship between a practitioner and a parent or caregiver is more likely to have optimal benefits when the parent sees himself or herself as an agent of change in achieving desired family-identified outcomes.*

clusters of practices (Trivette & Dunst, 1998). The relational component includes practices typically associated with: (1) good clinical skills (e.g., active listening, compassion, empathy, respect, being nonjudgmental); and (2) professional beliefs about and attitudes toward families, especially those pertaining to parenting capabilities and competencies. The participatory component includes practices that: (1) are individualized, flexible, and responsive to family concerns and priorities; and (2) provide families with opportunities to be actively involved in decisions and choices, family-professional collaboration, and family actions to achieve desired goals and outcomes. The simultaneous use of both sets of practices is what distinguishes a family-centered approach from other approaches to working with families (Dunst, 2002; Dunst & Trivette, 1996).

Family-Centered Practices Checklist

The Family-Centered Helpgiving Practices Model developed by Trivette and Dunst (1998) was used to develop a checklist for promoting early childhood practitioners' adoption of family-centered, competency-enhancing helpgiving practices. The "Family-Centered Practices Checklist" is used to determine the extent to which a practitioner uses both relational and participatory family-centered helpgiving practices as part of his or her work with a family.

The items on the Checklist were developed using several activities. Available research was reviewed (Trivette & Dunst, 1998, 2000), and both family support principles (Dunst, 1995) and parent comments about the characteristics of effective helpgivers were used to develop an item pool. The Checklist items then were compared to the indicators of evidence-based helpgiving practices to ensure that all aspects of family-centered practices were represented (Trivette & Dunst, 1998). A draft was distributed to practitioners to review and provide feedback about their use of the Checklist. Written and verbal feedback was solicited from practitioners and used to make the final selection of Checklist items. Practitioner feedback not only helped identify the items that best captured descriptions of helpgiving practices, but also helped improve the clarity of the Checklist.

The items on the Checklist are conceptually organized into the two components of family-centered practices (i.e., relational and participatory helpgiving practices). As mentioned previously, each component includes two clusters of helpgiving practices. In the following sections, we describe the components and clusters included on the Checklist. A blank copy of the Checklist, with instruction sheet, is included in the Appendix.

Relational Helpgiving Practices: Interpersonal Skills and Asset-Based Attitudes

Relational helpgiving practices are grouped into two clusters: interpersonal skills and asset-based attitudes. The interpersonal skills cluster includes behaviors that a practitioner uses to build rapport with parents and families. Practitioners demonstrate relational helpgiving by interacting with a family in a warm and caring way, focusing and maintaining attention on what a family member is saying, communicating clearly, and using active and reflective listening skills.

The second cluster of relational helpgiving behaviors includes practitioner behaviors that demonstrate a positive attitude toward the family. These behaviors include focusing on individual and family strengths, honoring and respecting personal and cultural beliefs, communicating to and about families in a positive way, and acknowledging the family's existing and emerging ability to achieve desired outcomes.

Participatory Helpgiving Practices: Family Choice and Action and Practitioner Responsiveness

Participatory helpgiving practices also are grouped into two clusters: family choice and action and practitioner responsiveness. The family choice and action cluster includes behaviors that a practitioner uses to assist families in making choices and taking action to achieve desired outcomes. Practitioners demonstrate participatory helpgiving by helping families to identify and focus on family-identified priorities, assisting families in the evaluation of options and in making informed decisions, promoting active family participation in the achievement of desired outcomes, and helping families use their existing strengths and building new skills to achieve those outcomes.

The practitioner responsiveness cluster includes behaviors that show responsiveness to families' unique and changing circumstances. A practitioner demonstrating responsiveness uses behaviors such as assisting families in considering solutions for desired outcomes that include a broad range of supports and resources, supporting and respecting family decisions, working with families in an individualized manner, offering help that matches family interests and priorities, and assisting families in taking a planned approach to achieving desired outcomes.

Administering the Checklist

The Checklist is completed based on an observation of a practitioner-family interaction, or as part of a conversation or description of a specific practitioner-family interaction. Each item is rated using the following scale: 1 = Yes, practice was used; 2 = Practice was partially, sometimes done; 3 = Practice not used, opportunity missed; 4 = NA, no opportunity to observe the practice. Examples of the practitioner's behavior are recorded in the spaces provided on the Checklist. The description of specific, observable behaviors aids in the discussion of and reflection on the characteristics of practices that are and are not indicators of family-centered helpgiving.

Feedback and Reflection

The Checklist provides standards and benchmarks for defining expected practitioner helpgiving behaviors and is useful for a number of purposes. First, a supervisor can use the Checklist to develop and support a practitioner's use of family-centered practices. For example, a supervisor can use the Checklist with a new employee to help the practitioner understand the key characteristics of family-centered practices and the behaviors expected in interactions with a family. The Checklist also can provide a means to structure supervisory observations of practitioner performance and subsequent discussions about a practitioner's use of family-centered practices.

Second, a practitioner can use the Checklist, either individually or with a coworker or coach, to reflect on and improve his or her helpgiving practices. For example, if a practitioner wanted to obtain feedback on his or her use of responsive and flexible helpgiving behaviors, he or she could have a coworker observe and record examples of this specific helpgiving practice that occur during an interaction with a family (e.g., ways the practitioner respected family decision making). The coworker could then use the observations to provide feedback or engage the practitioner in reflection.

There are a number of other potential uses for the Checklist. It can be used to capture key aspects of interactions with parents to help a practitioner examine whether or not he or she is using practices that promote a parent's active participation in achieving outcomes. It can be used by a practitioner to illustrate his or her helpgiving practices to other staff members or supervisors. It also can be used as an observation tool to capture and examine the interactions of two or more staff members working with one or more families. We have also found the

Checklist to be useful as a tool for structuring team conversations about many different aspects of family-centered helpgiving.

Examples of the Use of the Checklist

Two examples of the use of the Checklist follow. One example focuses on relational helpgiving practices and the other illustrates the use of participatory helpgiving.

Relational Helpgiving

Table 1 shows a completed Checklist for relational helpgiving practices. A coworker completed the Checklist based on an interaction between a practitioner (colleague) and a family. The coworker used the Checklist to record behaviors she observed and to complete the Checklist items. After the visit with the family was completed, the coworker used the Checklist to provide feedback, and both practitioners used the information to engage in a discussion and reflections about the helpgiving practices.

[The Checklist] can be used to capture key aspects of interactions with parents to help a practitioner examine whether or not he or she is using practices that promote a parent's active participation in achieving outcomes.

The coworker noted that the practitioner, Jane, listened attentively to the parents, showed sincere interest in what they were saying, discussed information with the family clearly, and interacted in a caring manner by asking the parents what they thought about their specific situation. The coworker also observed the practitioner's use of asset-based behaviors. She noted that the practitioner communicated somewhat positively about the child, but tended to concentrate on what the child wasn't capable of doing rather than on what the child was able to do. She also made an assumption about how the family wanted to work with their daughter. As part of discussing a therapist's role in the intervention process, Jane told the parents what she knew, but did not ask the parents what they hoped to achieve.

The coworker and practitioner discussed the interaction with each other immediately after the visit with the family. The coworker discussed the specific behaviors observed, and the extent to which helpgiving practices were consistent with Checklist items. The coworker made comments such as, "I noticed that you showed interest in what the parents had to say by your leaning forward and looking at the parents

Table 1: Example Relational Helpgiving Practices Items
Completed by a Coworker Using the "Family-Centered Practices Checklist"

Rating Scale		1=Yes, practice was used; 2=Practice was partially, sometimes done; 3=Practice not used, opportunity missed; 4=NA, no opportunity to observe the practice		
In what way was each practice used?			Rating	Example/Comment/Reflection
RELATIONAL PRACTICES	Interpersonal Skills	Listen to and understand family members' needs, concerns, and priorities	1	Jane looked at the parent; her body leaned forward to reflect interest in what the parent was saying.
		Communicate clear and complete information in a manner that matches the family's style and level of understanding	1	Jane was able to discuss and explain the assessment results. She provided examples to the family to assist their understanding; the family acknowledged that they understood the information.
		Interact with the family in a warm, caring, and empathetic manner	1	Jane discussed with the family the current evaluation. She asked what the family thought of the results. She nodded and continued to look at the parents.
		Treat the family with dignity and respect and without judgment	1	Jane introduced me at the beginning of the visit. She thanked the parents for letting me accompany her today.
	Asset-Based Attitudes	Communicate to and about the family in a positive way	3	Jane emphasized that the child was social but that she should be moving around more than she is (somewhat positive—redirected to what she wasn't doing).
		Honor and respect the family's personal and cultural beliefs and values	3	Jane assumed the parents would follow a certain approach to help their child. She didn't ask what they thought.
		Focus on individual and family strengths and assets	3	The conversation Jane and the family had centered on what the family needed to do more of to help their child to move; no mention of what the child was currently doing.
		Acknowledge the family's ability to achieve desired outcomes	2	Jane talked about the role of the OT and the role of the parents. She commented that she knew they could do it.

when they spoke." She also promoted discussion and reflection by saying, "I also noticed that you pointed out that the child was very social, but then you redirected the conversation to address the child's problem in being able to get around on his own. How was this in keeping with the asset-based component of relational helpgiving?" Both practitioners noted that when comments and behaviors were specific and concrete, they were better able to gain a deeper understanding of the characteristics of helpgiving practices.

The practitioners were both able to examine the specific practices and talk about what could have happened differently. By looking at the examples of her practices, Jane learned that she needed to communicate more positively than she had been and to focus on helping the family not only identify strengths, but also build on those strengths to achieve their desired outcomes. In this instance, the Checklist served as a useful tool to promote further discussion about the practices and provided the practitioner with specific information that she can use to become a more family-centered helpgiver.

Participatory Helpgiving

Table 2 shows a completed Checklist for participatory helpgiving practices. The Checklist was self-administered by a practitioner based on an interaction she had with a family. The focus of the practitioner-family interaction was to obtain information about the child's development, likes, and abilities. The practitioner recorded specific actions and behaviors she used with the family, and compared them to the family-centered helpgiving practice indicators. She concentrated mainly on her use of participatory helpgiving practices as they relate to promoting family choice and action.

The practitioner noted that she asked the family what they hoped to achieve from the visit, listened and asked questions to promote parent input and active participation, and encouraged the parents to share information about their child's strengths and abilities. She identified what the family knew about their child's likes and abilities, but did not point out how this information could be useful for achieving their desired outcomes. She also asked questions about the medical report the family had just received, but didn't follow up with them regarding what they wanted to do about their dissatisfaction with the report.

In this particular case, the practitioner used the Checklist as a tool to engage in self-reflection, sharpen her awareness and understanding of her practices, and determine whether her practices were consistent with participatory helpgiving behaviors. She discovered that she had

Table 2: Example Participatory Helpgiving Practices Items Self-Rated by a Practitioner Using the "Family-Centered Practices Checklist"

Rating Scale	1=Yes, practice was used; 2=Practice was partially, sometimes done; 3=Practice not used, opportunity missed; 4=NA, no opportunity to observe the practice		
In what way was each practice used?		Rating	Example/Comment/Reflection
PARTICIPATORY PRACTICES	Family Choice and Action		
		Work in partnership with parent(s)/family members to identify and address family-identified desires — 1	I asked the family what they wanted to get out of the visit today. I discussed the parents' thoughts and dissatisfaction with the results of the medical report they received.
		Encourage and assist the family to make decisions about and evaluate the resources best suited for achieving desired outcomes — 3	I listened to the parents. I didn't ask questions or discuss what the family wanted to do about the information they received/disagreed with.
		Seek and promote ongoing parent/family input and active participation regarding desired outcomes — 1	I asked questions about what the child could do and how the family spends their time. I used the parents as informants and participants in gathering information.
		Encourage and assist the family to use existing strengths and assets as a way of achieving desired outcomes — 2	I listened and asked the parents to tell me about what they know about their child.
		Provide family participatory opportunities to learn and develop new skills — 3	I asked questions but did not facilitate the parents' reflection on their thoughts about their child beyond their initial comments.
	Practitioner Responsiveness	Assist the family to consider solutions for desired outcomes that include a broad range of family and community supports and resources — 3	I asked the parents about their thoughts about the medical report, but then did not explore any options or sources of information with the family to address their dissatisfaction with the report.
		Support and respect family members' decisions — NA	
		Work with the family in a flexible and individualized manner — NA	
		Offer help that is responsive to and matches the family's interests and priorities — NA	
		Assist the family to take a positive, planful approach to achieving desired outcomes — NA	

difficulty going beyond the initial conversations with the parents and the initial comments that the parents made about their child and family. The practitioner recognized that she needed to pay attention to not only her ability to listen to what the family was saying, but also her ability to help the family explore and evaluate resources and to use the information they possess to make informed decisions. This self-reflection process helped the practitioner identify areas for improving her helpgiving practices.

Conclusion

How can one tell if a practitioner is using family-centered helpgiving practices? Let's return to the opening vignette. Martha, the early intervention practitioner working with Charlie's family, was engaged in an interaction to help the parent find child care for her son. An examination of the interaction using the "Family-Centered Practices Checklist" shows that Martha listened to the mother's desires, interacted with the mother in a warm and caring manner, and was respectful of the family's lifestyle. This indicates that Martha was using practices consistent with the relational helpgiving indicators. But what about participatory helpgiving practices? Martha did share information about two child care programs, but suggested that the mother consider the one Martha thought best for Charlie. Martha also acted on the mother's behalf by saying she would arrange a visit to the center. These are examples of missed opportunities to engage the mother in evaluating choices, making decisions, and acting on the decisions. Doing things for people may seem helpful, but such actions are sure signs of a dependency-forming style of helpgiving that is not consistent with family-centered practices (Rappaport, 1981).

Tools like the "Family-Centered Practices Checklist" can be helpful as a way of making concrete and practical the kinds of behaviors that mirror a family-centered approach (Trivette & Dunst, 2000). It also provides a context for joint or self-reflection as a way of checking one's helpgiving behaviors against a set of behaviorally stated, evidence-based standards. How do your helpgiving practices stand up against the indicators on the scale? Checking out your practices using the "Family-Centered Practices Checklist" can help you answer this important question.

Appendix

Family-Centered Practices Checklist

Practitioner _____   Context _____

Observer/Coach _____   Date(s) _____

Rating Scale: 1=Yes, practice was used; 2=Practice was partially, sometimes done; 3=Practice not used, opportunity missed; 4=NA, no opportunity to observe the practice

RELATIONAL PRACTICES	In what way was each practice used?	Rating	Example/Comment/Reflection
Interpersonal Skills	Listen to and understand family members' needs, concerns, and priorities		
	Communicate clear and complete information in a manner that matches the family's style and level of understanding		
	Interact with the family in a warm, caring, and empathetic manner		
	Treat the family with dignity and respect and without judgment		
Asset-Based Attitudes	Communicate to and about the family in a positive way		
	Honor and respect the family's personal and cultural beliefs and values		
	Focus on individual and family strengths and assets		
	Acknowledge the family's ability to achieve desired outcomes		

Appendix: Family-Centered Practices Checklist (continued)

PARTICIPATORY PRACTICES		In what way was each practice used?	Rating	Example/Comment/Reflection
Family Choice and Action		Work in partnership with parent(s)/family members to identify and address family-identified desires		
		Encourage and assist the family to make decisions about and evaluate the resources best suited for achieving desired outcomes		
		Seek and promote ongoing parent/family input and active participation regarding desired outcomes		
		Encourage and assist the family to use existing strengths and assets as a way of achieving desired outcomes		
		Provide family participatory opportunities to learn and develop new skills		
Practitioner Responsiveness		Assist the family to consider solutions for desired outcomes that include a broad range of family and community supports and resources		
		Support and respect family members' decisions		
		Work with the family in a flexible and individualized manner		
		Offer help that is responsive to and matches the family's interests and priorities		
		Assist the family to take a positive, planful approach to achieving desired outcomes		

Copyright © 2002 by the Family, Infant, and Preschool Program, Western Carolina Center, Morganton, NC. This checklist may be reproduced for practice purposes.

Appendix: Family-Centered Practices Checklist (continued)

The "Family-Centered Practices Checklist" is used to determine the extent to which a practitioner uses family-centered helpgiving practices. The Checklist includes items based on characteristics of effective family-centered helpgiving practices, and captures both relational and participatory helpgiving behaviors (Trivette & Dunst, 1998). Relational helpgiving practices include a helpgiver's interpersonal skills with families and his or her attitudes and beliefs about the family's skills and ability to become more competent. Participatory helpgiving practices include helpgiver behaviors that promote family choice and action as well as helpgiver practices that are flexible and responsive to the family's priorities and interests.

The Checklist can be used for several purposes. It can be used by supervisors to: (1) inform newly hired practitioners about family-centered practices and the behavioral expectations for their interactions with families, and (2) structure observations of practitioner performance and discussions about his or her use of family-centered practices. Practitioners also can use the scale, either individually or with a coworker or coach, to self-assess, reflect on, and improve their practices with families.

The Checklist is administered during an observation of a practitioner-family interaction, or as part of self-reflection on a specific interaction with a family. Information is completed regarding: (1) the date of the observation or self-reflection; (2) the context of the practitioner-family interaction (e.g., initial contact with the family, IFSP development, identifying a child's interests, reviewing progress toward desired outcomes, etc.); (3) the name of the practitioner being observed or conducting the self-assessment; and (4) the name of the person conducting the observation (if applicable). Each item is rated using the following scale:

1 = Yes, practice was used

2 = Practice was partially, sometimes done

3 = Practice not used, opportunity missed

4 = NA, no opportunity to observe the practice

An observable example of the behavior, and/or comments on practitioner behavior, are written in the "Example/Comment/Reflection section" of the Checklist.

When using the "Family-Centered Practices Checklist" to provide feedback to others or to further one's own understanding of the practices, consider the following: (1) review the items and discuss the behaviors observed, (2) identify a specific item or set of items that will be the focus of discussion or reflection, (3) describe the characteristics of the practice and what it is about the behavior observed that represents family-centered practice, (4) describe the context of the interaction, (5) describe the results of the interaction, (6) reflect on the practice and describe what if anything the practitioner could have done differently, and (7) identify and describe how the practice complemented or contradicted another family-centered practice within the example being discussed.

Reference
Trivette, C. M., & Dunst, C. J. (1998, December). *Family-centered helpgiving practices.* Paper presented at the 14th Annual Division for Early Childhood International Conference on Children With Special Needs, Chicago.

Notes

The authors acknowledge the contributions of the staff of the Family, Infant, and Preschool Program, and especially Melinda Raab and Deb Batman, who assisted in the development and refinement of the "Family-Centered Practices Checklist."

You can reach Linda L. Wilson by e-mail at Linda.Wilson@westerncarolinacenter.org

References

Davies, D. (1995). Collaboration and family empowerment as strategies to achieve comprehensive services. In L. C. Rigsby, M. C. Reynolds, & M. C. Wang (Eds.), *School-community connections: Exploring issues for research and practice* (pp. 267-280). San Francisco: Jossey-Bass.

Dunst, C. J. (1995). *Key characteristics and features of community-based family support programs.* Chicago: Family Resource Coalition.

Dunst, C. J. (2002). Family-centered practices: Birth through high school. *Journal of Special Education, 36,* 139-147.

Dunst, C. J., & Trivette, C. M. (1996). Empowerment, effective helpgiving practices, and family-centered care. *Pediatric Nursing, 22,* 334-337, 343.

Family, Infant, and Preschool Program. (2002). *Family-centered practices checklist.* Morganton, NC: Author.

Rappaport, J. (1981). In praise of paradox: A social policy of empowerment over prevention. *American Journal of Community Psychology, 9,* 1-25.

Shelton, T. L., & Stepanak, J. S. (1994). *Family-centered care for children needing specialized health and developmental services* (2nd ed.). Bethesda, MD: Association for the Care of Children's Health.

Trivette, C. M., & Dunst, C. J. (1998, December). *Family-centered helpgiving practices.* Paper presented at the 14th Annual Division for Early Childhood International Conference on Children With Special Needs, Chicago.

Trivette, C. M., & Dunst, C. J. (2000). Recommended practices in family-based practices. In S. Sandall, M. E. McLean, & B. J. Smith (Eds.), *DEC recommended practices in early intervention/early childhood special education* (pp. 39-46). Longmont, CO: Sopris West.

Honoring Differences

Essential Features of Appropriate ECSE Services for Young Children From Diverse Sociocultural Environments

---

Isaura Barrera, Ph.D.,
University of New Mexico

As Shelton (1999) stated, "… the more closely we examine a complex problem, the fuzzier its solution is likely to be" (p. 49). It is easy to become overwhelmed as one examines the practical implications of providing appropriate ECSE services to culturally- linguistically diverse (CLD) children and families (i.e., children and families who: [1] speak language[s] other than English at home; and/or [2] have values, beliefs, understandings, and practices different from those considered normative in ECSE literature and settings). Despite all the attention paid to the presence of diverse cultures and languages in ECSE settings during the past ten years, there remains a need to explore the application of recommended practices to concrete situations in which resources may be limited and family characteristics different from those described in the literature. The purpose of this article is to share specific service features that can help programs honor differences in all situations, even when resources are significantly limited. These service features were initially identified and successfully piloted during the three-year implementation of "CROSSROADS," a federally funded demonstration program that provided technical assistance to ECSE programs on services for children with special needs from culturally-linguistically diverse backgrounds (Barrera & Hoot, 1990). They also have been cross-referenced to current theory and research.

Service Features

Through the implementation of "CROSSROADS," six program features were found to help programs honor cultural-linguistic differences. These features are especially important because of their accessibility to any program in any area, however remote or isolated. They are not dependent upon finding fully trained personnel, *though they do not replace the need for such personnel*. Honoring the rich differences that children and families bring to ECSE programs should not be dependent on a specific level of resources, but rather should be the practice in every program, even as efforts continue to increase resources and prepare personnel.

Feature #1: Recognizing the Pervasive Influence of Culture and Cultural Dynamics

The experience of "CROSSROADS" staff over three years and eight different programs substantiated the importance of focusing on what culture is and how it tends to operate in families. Cultural identities are relevant and valid in relation to all families and children precisely because culture is a pervasive reality. All of us see individuals and all else in the world around us through culturally-tinted lenses (i.e., through the conceptual and behavioral templates we have adopted, both consciously and unconsciously). The words we use and the categories we tend to perceive are largely the result of the culture(s) in which we participate. Children raised in the Navajo tradition, for example, are exposed to dramatically different perceptions and conceptualizations of time than are children raised within other cultural traditions. This exposure may not be consciously directed. Its presence may, in fact, not be conscious at all, but may be embedded in the pace and structure of daily activities and expectations surrounding them (Cole, 1996; Greenfield, 1994).

The purpose of recognizing culture and cultural dynamics is not to predict or anticipate. *It is, rather, to become open and respectful to diverse behaviors even when these are outside of our areas of familiarity.* In effect, such recognition expands our appreciation of how truly unique all individuals are. Langer (1989) discusses this apparent paradox: "These efforts [to combat prejudice by reducing categorization] are based on the view that, in an ideal world, everyone should be considered equal, falling under the single category of 'human being'" (p. 154). She suggests "… a different approach to combating prejudice—one in which we learn to make more, rather than fewer, distinctions among people" (p. 154). That way the likelihood that someone's identity can be defined by a single category is greatly reduced.

The purpose of recognizing culture and cultural dynamics is not to predict or anticipate. It is, rather, to become open and respectful to diverse behaviors even when these are outside of our areas of familiarity.

In working with programs to respond to children's and families' needs, "CROSSROADS" staff identified various issues that came up repeatedly as programs explored how to honor cultural-linguistic diversity. These issues could be grouped into three inter-related dimensions reflective of their content: (1) communicative-linguistic (i.e., issues related to how we communicate and inter-

act); (2) sensory-cognitive (i.e., issues of what and how we know); and (3) personal-social (i.e., issues related to power, identity, and sense of self) (see Table 1). Many of the challenges to honoring differences faced by the programs with which "CROSSROADS" staff worked were related to diversity between family perspectives on these issues and practitioner/program perspectives.

Communicative-Linguistic Dimension

Differences in the language(s) used in the child's primary caregiving environment(s) and language(s) used by ECSE practitioners were, of course, an obvious challenge. Another, more subtle, challenge resulted from differences in the relative value placed on verbal and nonverbal communication (e.g., ECSE objectives might emphasize oral vocabulary, while family members placed more value on appropriate nonverbal communication, such as silence when elders were speaking). An interesting discussion about these more subtle challenges can be found in Bowers and Flinders (1990).

Sensory-Cognitive Dimension

Differences in the aspects of situations, persons, and objects that families or practitioners deemed most important, what Moll and Greeberg (1990) term "funds of know-ledge," also presented significant challenges to collaboration and communication between practitioners and families. A mother might, for example, know and care a great deal about her daughter's social abilities, but might focus much less on her ability to finish a three-piece form puzzle, and might in fact be puzzled herself about why an ECSE practitioner finds this task so significant. Rothstein-Fisch (1998) provides several excellent examples of these challenges in relation to kindergarten situations.

Personal-Social Dimension

A third source of challenges can be clustered into the personal-social dimension, which addresses not what we know but who we are. One common difference involved varying perspectives on "autonomy" and the degree of parent-child separation that this entails. Family beliefs and practices often differed significantly from those of practitioners in this area, especially in relation to the degree of comfort with assistance given to children completing a task.

Table 1 lists other specific areas within each dimension in which differences were likely to be evident and present a challenge. Clarification of and responsiveness to these differences was an important strategy for honoring diversity. The remaining features address a range of specific strategies that "CROSSROADS" staff used to help programs honor diverse perspectives within each of these three dimensions. (Additional information on the specific areas can be obtained from Barrera, Corso, & Macpherson, 2003.)

Feature #2: Increasing Access Between Families and Services

Once culture is acknowledged as an educationally valid construct for all children, one of the major hurdles in serving diverse children with special needs and their families is access—both access to services by the families (i.e., knowing where services are and how to get them), and access to the families by the practitioners (i.e., knowing how to reach CLD populations and getting appropriate information to them). Implementation of the "CROSSROADS" program yielded data indicating the importance of oral, face-to-face contact in increasing families' access to ECSE services across a variety of cultural-linguistic groups. This was often not a simple matter of literacy. Many families placed more credibility on oral communication than on written communication; or they simply found it more familiar and preferable, regardless of their level of literacy. One way of disseminating information orally that proved to be highly effective was to contact significant persons in particular neighborhoods or areas where there were concentrations of diverse populations. These persons included clergy, respected community leaders, and staff from other agencies.

The degree of credibility established by ECSE programs and practitioners was also found to influence access. Many families had had negative experiences with "friendly intruders" (e.g., social workers, medical personnel). Some families had no familiarity with service providers and, thus, no script for interacting with them; other families had scripts that

Table 1: Specific Areas Particularly Sensitive to Culture and
Cultural Dynamics

Communicative-Linguistic

1. Language(s) of the child's primary caregiving environment(s)

2. Child's relative language proficiency (degree of proficiency in all languages used)

3. Patterns of language usage in child's primary caregiving environment(s) (e.g., What is each language used for? Who says what to whom? In what language?)

4. Relative value placed on verbal and nonverbal communication, both explicit (when asked) and implicit (when observed)

5. Relative status associated with non-English language and bilingualism, both explicit and implicit (i.e., Does the family speak a language that is highly valued by nonspeakers? Is bilingualism seen as an asset or a risk?)

Sensory-Cognitive

1. Funds of knowledge (i.e., What knowledge and concepts are valued? What types of information are familiar to the family? Are funds of knowledge primarily personal and familial? Communal? Institutionalized?)

2. Preferred strategies for acquiring new learning (e.g., verbal over nonverbal, modeling or reading)

3. Preferred strategies for problem solving and decision making (e.g., interpersonal, linear, circular, individual or communal)

4. World view (i.e., assumptions about how the world works, about "right" and "wrong"; how events are explained and understood)

Personal-Social

1. Degree of family's acculturation into culture(s) other than the one they identify as primary

2. Degree of acculturation into US "professional" culture (e.g., health professions, ECSE)

3. Construction of sense of self (e.g., relative weight given to self-reliance as compared to social referencing, value placed on autonomy as compared to interdependence)

4. Family structure and process (e.g., Who is designated as primary authority figure[s]? What roles tend to be adopted?)

5. Perceptions of identity and competence (e.g., What characteristics define competence?)

6. Knowledge and experience related to power and social positioning

7. Values and beliefs associated with obtaining and providing support for adults and children

were not applicable to the particular settings in which they now found themselves. Practitioners were often total strangers seeking to obtain information not typically given to total strangers by members of any culture. In addition, practitioners did not always speak the families' home language(s) and sometimes behaved in unpredictable or unacceptable ways from the families' perspectives. All of these issues were compounded by families' previous experiences with services that were more discontinuous than continuous (e.g., not seeing the same person twice).

Establishing personal and programmatic credibility involved being willing to enter into extended and reciprocal relationships within which personal information was given as well as requested. Practitioners were at times asked, "Are you married?" or "Do you have any children?" In professional settings, these questions may be perceived as intrusive, or as trying to establish a personal relationship instead of a professional one. Far from being intrusive, however, such questioning came to be considered a way of assessing values and beliefs (i.e., as a way of coming to know who a person was and how best to relate to them). From this perspective, these questions helped families to build a common bond with ECSE practitioners rather than a "one-up, one-down" connection often established by coming into a home as the professional expert or helper.

Feature #3: Recognizing the Importance of Establishing Rapport

The dictionary defines rapport as "relation marked by harmony, conformity, accord, or affinity" (Mirriam-Webster, 1999). The experience of "CROSSROADS" staff indicated that, once contact was made with families and general information given, establishing rapport must become an essential feature of service delivery.

Rapport tends to be most easily established when one person involved feels that the other person both understands his or her point of view, and validates that point of view in some way (Brooks, 1989). When serving children and families whose cultural parameters and language(s) are different from those of the ECSE program or staff, however, there is a strong probability that experiential and conceptual perspectives will be dissimilar. Thus, establishing rapport may not occur as easily; it may require careful and explicit attention. Adults and children entering new and unfamiliar arenas often scan unconsciously for clues to the question "Do you know how I feel?" and then respond accordingly (Anderson, 1999). There were two keys to facilitating rapport in these instances. The first was an understanding of the stress that often accompanies learning new cultural parameters and language(s) (Igoa, 1995). This stress can arise from one or more of the following:

1. The subjective experience of being, or being perceived as, different or an outsider.
2. The psychological experience of finding that one is no longer competent at things that, in other settings, one has already mastered (e.g., giving a compliment, asking a question).
3. The loss/grief that may accompany decreased access to familiar places and persons.
4. The role reversal that can happen as parents and other adults lag behind children in various areas of adaptation and learning, such as language.
5. The loss of authority and credibility that can occur as children reject the old ways in favor of new ones.

Recognition of these factors was communicated to the family both verbally and nonverbally through a variety of strategies such as those described in Feature #4.

The second key to facilitating rapport was effective and responsive communication. All too often families from diverse cultural backgrounds are expected to do all the necessary adaptation (e.g., learn English, bring an interpreter, explain their culture) at the same time that they are dealing with the stress of having suspected delays or disabilities confirmed. Use of home language(s); nonjudgmental acceptance of diverse behaviors; the presence of someone with whom the family could identify; adaptation of procedures to avoid negative perceptions (e.g., not asking direct personal questions such as, "Did you breastfeed your child?" in the initial interview)—all these behaviors and other similar ones were used to communicate both respect and acceptance.

Responsive communication requires recognition of potential "culture bumps" (Archer, 1986; Barrera, 1989). A culture bump is a behavior or situation that is experienced negatively because it is perceived, consciously or unconsciously, to be in conflict with the observer's own values, beliefs, or expectations. The family or child and the practitioner(s) figuratively "bump up against" something and feel jostled or disturbed to a greater or lesser degree. Culture bumps were anticipated and adjusted for by reviewing similarities and differences between families and practitioners in the areas listed in Feature #1. Common strategies included checking ahead of time on whether specific arrangements were likely to communicate respect or disrespect to families from a particular background, ensuring that program staff communicated in ways that made sense within a family's values and belief system (e.g., using an indirect style instead of a direct style for making requests), and drawing on families' funds of knowledge (Moll & Greeberg, 1990) when explaining children's strengths and limitations (e.g., using familiar terms and scenarios).

Feature #4: Supporting Families' Efforts to Deal With Diverse Culture(s) and Language(s)

Few families come into ECSE programs and explicitly state, "We are culturally-linguistically diverse and desire support and adaptation of your procedures." "CROSSROADS" staff were aware, from their own experiences and from conversations with families, that there could be some degree of shame connected with being less than proficient in English or with being insufficiently familiar with the culture reflected in the ECSE program. It was decided, therefore, that the practitioners should bear primary responsibility for identifying the role that culture and language played in a particular situation, and should then provide the necessary support. While it was recognized that families often needed to acquire proficiency in English and learn to function competently in the setting(s) in which they found themselves, it also was recognized that they did not necessarily need to do so while addressing their child's delay/disability and negotiating the special education process.

One effective means of providing family support was the use of "Parent Partners": paraprofessionals and volunteers fluent in a family's language and culture whose responsibility it was to be with the family during key times such as home visits, clinic visits, assessments, and meetings with ECSE personnel. The goal of Parent Partners was to mediate between familiar and unfamiliar aspects of a particular situation, while also helping the family to negotiate these aspects on their own subsequently. One Parent Partner, for example, assisted a young mother who had to come in for an assessment and did not have transportation or speak much English. She went to the mother's home and showed her how to call for a Medicaid-paid taxi, something the mother had never done. This mother had also expressed some anxiety about getting into a cab driven by a stranger since she had little experience going out unaccompanied. The Parent Partner accompanied her on her first trip, showing her how to give written directions to the driver. For her second trip, the Parent Partner went to her home and followed the taxi to the appointment site. By the third trip, the mother was comfortable just being met at the site by the Parent Partner. She could now get to appointments by herself, and had new confidence in her ability to learn and negotiate unfamiliar situations. This mother was soon helping other parents with the same difficulties she initially had experienced.

Feature #5: Developing Reciprocal "Additive" Responses to Families and Children

ECSE services and settings can respond to culturally-linguistically diverse children and families in either a subtractive fashion or an additive, reciprocal fashion (Cummins & McNeely, 1987). Subtractive responses carry an implicit or explicit message that the old must be left behind so that the new can replace it (e.g., families must suspend the use of Spanish in order for their child to learn English). Additive responses, on the other hand, do not see a conflict between existing and new behaviors; they support the   addition of new information or behaviors to the old. In this type of response, practitioners respect the linguistic and behavioral repertoire of the children and their families and seek to expand rather than limit it. Adaptation efforts are accepted with the understanding that acculturation is a highly complex and often stressful process requiring time and risk-taking. Rather than favoring professional expertise over families' experiences, additive responses view interactions as a two-way process in which the parties are each responsive to and shaped by the other. Rules within this response system therefore tend to recognize a more equal distribution of knowledge and to define relationships more personally.

Reciprocity, however, does not imply that change is unnecessary. To reduce it to those terms does a tremendous disservice to everyone concerned. *The real issue addressed by this feature is the degree to which practitioners equalize and distribute power, and then communicate to children and families that their home language and culture are a valuable asset, rather than a liability.* It is this message that was found to be key. Once it was in place, families' confidence in their ability to participate as equal partners in making decisions about language usage and acculturation increased noticeably.

Feature #6: Addressing the Need for Cultural-Linguistic Mediation

Greenberg and Kaniel (1990) state that a " ... significant variable in cultural transition is mediated learning" (p. 139). The term mediation in this context refers to " ... the way in which stimuli emitted by the environment are transformed by a 'mediating' agent, usually a parent, sibling, or other caregiver .... The mediator selects stimuli that are most appropriate and then frames, filters, and schedules them ... " (Feuerstein, 1980, pp. 16-17). Data from "CROSSROADS" indicated two reasons making mediation necessary when providing services to children and families whose cultural parameters and language were diverse from practitioners'.

The first reason related to the family's need to negotiate unfamiliar values, beliefs, behaviors, and expectations (i.e., cultures). Existing mediation skills often become inappropriate or ineffective for both children and family members when cultural contexts change, as happens between home and school for culturally-linguistically diverse children. In addition, when contexts change beyond our ability to mediate them, feelings of failure, inadequacy, and/or incompetence may result. The experience of no longer being competent at something one has previously mastered (e.g., asking for help) can have both cognitive and psychological ramifications, especially for young children just developing their sense of self and competence (Skutnabb-Kangas & Cummins, 1988). "CROSSROADS" practitioners, understanding the process of mediation and recognizing its importance, developed specific mediation strategies to help children and families learn new skills while minimizing or eliminating feelings of incompetence. For example, information was often broken down into smaller bits; unfamiliar cultural expectations were explicitly discussed and explained; and coping strategies, such as using tape recorders at medical appointments, were explicitly taught.

The second reason related to mediation across languages, which while a component of culture, merits separate attention. Language is a primary mediation tool; most of us use language to frame and filter stimuli, as well as to interact with others. It is difficult, if not impossible, to think about something or negotiate a situation when one does not have the necessary language. Westby (1985) said that one cannot learn a language and learn through that language at the same time. The focus of the two processes is simply too different. When one is learning a language, one's focus tends to be on simple decoding (e.g., if one cannot be sure whether someone is describing a horse or a house, it is difficult to learn *what* is being said about the subject, and if one is still trying to figure out what was just said, one cannot listen well to the sentences that follow that initial utterance).

One effective way "CROSSROADS" staff found to provide necessary culture and language mediation even when there was limited access to practitioners fluent in the child's home language and culture was through the use of language-culture "mediators" or brokers. Language-culture mediators were persons who could go between two or more languages or cultures: buffering differences, explaining the unfamiliar, and, in general, making one comprehensible to the other. Language-culture mediators were familiar with the three dimensions of behavior and learning that were determined to be particularly vulnerable (as described in Feature

#1). They learned to examine the areas within each dimension for possible cultural or linguistic dissonance and miscommunications (see Barrera, 1996; Barrera, Corso, & Macpherson, 2003; Barrera & Kramer, 1997). Ideally, ECSE practitioners themselves assumed the role of language-culture mediators with the support of "CROSSROADS" staff; when this was not possible, persons were brought in from other settings (e.g., community centers, churches). The term "mediator" was selected over "translator" or "interpreter" for two reasons. First, a mediator's role is broader that just translating and interpreting verbal language. Second, it is important to recognize that translating and interpreting are highly complex skills that require not just a knowledge of particular vocabulary, but also extensive familiarity with and understanding of the cultural context(s) from which that vocabulary derives meaning.

The role of language-culture mediators in "CROSSROADS" was twofold: (1) to assist ECSE practitioners in becoming aware of and responsive to the values, behaviors, and rules that are typical within a particular family's cultural context(s); and (2) to assist the family in becoming familiar with and negotiating the values, behaviors, and rules common to the ECSE service system and to special education in general. This latter role required that, if persons other than ECSE practitioners were employed as mediators, practitioners spend time familiarizing them with activities and procedures. "CROSSROADS" language-culture mediators enacted their roles through many different activities: being Parent Partners, translating, participating in staff training activities, and working to establish curricula. It was their goal to bridge familiar and unfamiliar cultures and languages.

Perspective, Patience, and Process

As O'Conner (1987) states, "We cannot have dialogue unless we honor the differences"(p. 39). There is sometimes a tendency to believe that, when optimum services cannot be provided, little *can* be done until such services are secured. As a result, practitioners may overlook all that *can* be done even while continuing to search for better alternatives. Honoring cultural differences may, then, require a shift in practitioners' perspectives as well as a critical review of values and assumptions reflected in typical ECSE settings, materials, and procedures. The service features discussed here provide some ideas, based on one program's efforts and experiences, of how this could be done. They provide a

We cannot have dialogue unless we honor the differences ....

perspective within which honoring cultural-linguistic differences can, with patience, become an ongoing process.

Note

Additional resources are available from the author via e-mail. You can reach Isaura Barrera by e-mail at ibarr@unm.edu

References

Anderson, P. (1999, March 26). *Discussion on culture.* Paper presented at meeting of Culturally & Linguistically Appropriate Services, Early Childhood Research Institute, San Diego, CA.

Archer, C. M. (1986). Culture bumps and beyond. In J. M. Valdes (Ed.), *Culture bound: Bridging the cultural gap in language teaching.* New York: Cambridge University Press.

Barrera, I. (1989). *Honoring the differences.* Unpublished monograph produced for CROSSROADS #G008730274, Department of Education, Office of Special Education, CFDA 94.024.

Barrera, I. (1996, May 1). *Two cultures, two languages: What do I do?* Unpublished material presented at Early Childhood Intervention Statewide Conference, Austin, TX.

Barrera, I., Corso, R., & Macpherson, D. (2003). *Skilled dialogue: Strategies for responding to cultural diversity in early childhood.* Baltimore: Paul H. Brookes.

Barrera, I., & Hoot, J. (1990). *Final grant report.* CROSSROADS #G008730274, Department of Education, Office of Special Education, CFDA 94.024.

Barrera, I., & Kramer, L. (1997). From monologues to skilled dialogues: Teaching the process of crafting culturally competent early childhood environments. In P. J. Winton, J. A. McCollum, & C. Catlett (Eds.), *Reforming personnel preparation in early intervention* (pp. 217-252). Baltimore: Paul H. Brookes.

Bowers, C. A., & Flinders, D. J. (1990). *Responsive teaching: An ecological approach to classroom patterns of language, culture, and thought.* New York: Teachers College Press.

Brooks, M. (1989). *Instant rapport.* New York: Warner.

Cole, M. (1996). *Cultural psychology.* Cambridge: Belknap Press.

Cummins, J., & McNeely, S. N. (1987). Language development, academic learning, and empowering minority students. In S. H. Fradd & W. J. Tikunoff (Eds.), *Bilingual education and bilingual special education* (pp. 75-97). Boston: College-Hill.

Feuerstein, R. (1980). *Instrumental enrichment.* Baltimore: University Park Press.

Greenberg, K. H., & Kaniel, S. (1990). A thousand year transition for Ethiopian immigrants to Israel: The effects of modifiability, mediated learning and cultural transmission. *International Journal of Cognitive Education & Mediated Learning, 1*(2), 137-142.

Greenfield, P. M. (1994). Independence and interdependence as developmental scripts: Implications for theory, research, and practice. In P. M. Greenfield & R. R. Cocking (Eds.), *Cross-cultural roots of minority child development* (pp. 1-37). Hillsdale, NJ: Lawrence Erlbaum.

Igoa, C. (1995). *The inner world of the immigrant child.* New York: St. Martin's Press.

Langer, E. J. (1989). *Mindfulness.* Menlo Park, CA: Addison-Wesley.

Mirriam-Webster. (Ed.). (1999, October 5). *Mirriam-Webster online dictionary.* Available from http://www.m-w.com

Moll, L. C., & Greeberg, J. B. (1990). Creating zones of possibilities: Combining social contexts for instruction. In L. C. Moll (Ed.), *Vygotsky and education: Instructional applications of sociohistorical psychology.* New York: Cambridge University Press.

O'Conner, E. (1987). *Cry pain, cry hope.* Waco, TX: Word.

Rothstein-Fisch, C. (1998). *Bridging cultures: A pre-service teacher preparation module.* San Francisco: WestEd.

Shelton, C. (1999). *Quantum leaps.* Woburn, MA: Butterworth-Heinemann.

Skutnabb-Kangas, T., & Cummins, J. (1988). *Minority education: From shame to struggle.* Philadelphia: Multilingual Matters.

Westby, C. E. (1985). Learning to talk—talking to learn. In C. S. Simon (Ed.), *Communication skills and classroom success* (pp. 181-218). San Diego, CA: College-Hill.

Partnerships With Family Members:

What About Fathers?

Linda L. Flynn-Wilson, Ph.D.,
University of New Orleans

Philip G. Wilson, Ph.D.,
University of New Orleans

Family-centered services and supports in early intervention/early childhood special education (EI/ECSE) include all family members. Researchers and service providers often conceptualize families as systems. This approach to understanding how families function is referred to as "family systems theory." Family systems theory assumes that families have their own way of approaching events in life, communicating among and between one another, determining rules for structure and change, and interacting with external organizations and individuals (Lambie & Daniels-Mohring, 1993). According to family systems theory, no individual can be understood outside the context of the family, and all families have productive and nonproductive interactions (Lambie & Daniels-Mohring, 1993). Additionally, socioeconomic conditions and cultural beliefs and practices of a family are critical influences on each family system.

Fathers are a critical member of the family system who influence their children and their families in unique ways. Typically, the concerns and priorities of mothers are the focus when teachers, nurses, therapists, and other service providers work with families who have children with disabilities, with little or no direct input from fathers. Service providers are challenged to learn more about fathers, their perspectives of their children, their roles within the family, and the nature of their relationships within the family.

Generally, we know that men approach problems differently than women (Davis & May, 1991). Women have a tendency to want to talk about the issues, whereas men often move directly to solving problems.

We also know that fathers interact and play differently with their children than do mothers (Lamb, 1986). For example, when given a pile of blocks, mothers often work together with their child to create a structure. Fathers, on the other hand, tend to say to the child, for example, "Here are your blocks and here are mine. Let's see who can build the tallest tower."

We know that a father's response to having a child with a disability is likely to be different than a mother's (Davis & May, 1991). A father might set aside his emotional response and move immediately into developing an action plan for his child. Conversely, the mother might go to the phone and call a relative to share her feelings about her child's disability. As members of the family system, fathers are critical players in their child's life. Therefore, it is imperative that service providers seek input, and active, ongoing involvement from fathers, as well as mothers, in EI/ECSE efforts.

Relationship and Interaction With Children

There are a number of benefits for children, fathers, and the family in general when fathers participate actively in child rearing (Frey, Fewell, & Vadasy, 1989; Hornby, 1992; Lamb, Pleck, Charnov, & Levine, 1987; Pruett, 1993). It appears that the closer the relationship a father has with his children, the better understanding he has of them (Lamb et al., 1987). For example, a father who picks his child up at child care and reads to his child is more likely to develop a close relationship with his child than a father who is not present and active in the everyday events of his child's life. Fathers who actively and regularly participate in their children's lives will also have a better understanding of their children's likes and dislikes. Additionally, a father who understands his child is more likely to feel competent in caring for the child and is more likely to experience personal satisfaction from his relationship with his child (Lamb et al., 1987).

> ... [A] father who understands his child is more likely to feel competent in caring for the child and is more likely to experience personal satisfaction from his relationship with his child ....

Fathers who are actively involved in their child's life are considered to be more accepting and have higher expectations of their child (Frey et al., 1989). For instance, fathers who participate in domestic routines (e.g., dressing), leisure activities (e.g., completing art projects), and learning/enrichment experiences (e.g., trips to libraries) may have more positive perceptions of their children with disabilities. In addition, fathers who are involved with their children who have disabilities report that this involvement contributes to "meaningfulness" in their own lives (Hornby, 1992). In  fact, fathers who are engaged with their children report greater personal happiness and have fewer signs of physical illness (Pruett, 1993).

There is also increasing evidence that a father's expectations and acceptance of his child with disabilities may play a significant role in determining the family's attitudes toward the child (McLinden, 1990). When a father feels positive about his child with disabilities, other family members may be more likely to adopt that same attitude.

Children's daily living skills and social skills are more advanced when the father's perception of the child is positive (Frey et al., 1989). It is hypothesized that fathers' positive perceptions lead to more interaction with their children and, thus, promote child competence. For example, we know that a father's active involvement with his child facilitates the child's ability to problem-solve (Easterbrooks & Goldberg, 1984). Positive child behaviors may also be due, in part, to the manner in which fathers tend to interact with their children. Lamb (1986) found that children without disabilities, particularly boys, who had positive relationships with their fathers, tended to have higher achievement, motivation, cognitive competence, better social skills, and a clearer identification with their gender.

A father's interaction stimulates the child's curiosity and problem-solving skills, and encourages independence which, in turn, enhances cognitive development (Pruett, 1993). For instance, if a father is working outside in his garden, he may give his child a tool with which to dig, a package of seeds and a watering can and encourage the child to plant his own garden. This activity can facilitate independence (e.g., the child's own tools and garden spot in which to work) and problem-solving skills (e.g., where and how to plant the seeds), as

A father's interaction stimulates the child's curiosity and problem-solving skills, and encourages independence ....

well as encourage the child to ask questions such as, "How do seeds grow?"

A father's interaction with his child may impact the child's development in other ways. Fathers tend to serve as a playmate for their children and "rough-house" with their children (Parke, 1988). Rough-housing may promote the child's motor development. For example, a child may reach out and stabilize her body during energetic play which, in turn, may facilitate the child's ability to integrate physical movement and position in space.

Fathers' style of interacting with their children has the potential to positively influence their children's development. The family system may be enhanced when fathers are actively involved in daily activities with their children. One goal for service providers may be to ensure that parents understand the importance of fathers' interaction with their children with disabilities and the value of gender-specific approaches to play and interaction. Many fathers may not naturally get involved, but if mothers and service providers encourage participation, fathers may be more likely to choose to participate. When fathers are not expected to play a primary role, a self-fulfilling prophecy may occur.

One goal for service providers may be to ensure that parents understand the importance of fathers' interaction with their children with disabilities and the value of gender-specific approaches to play and interaction.

Concerns and Priorities of Fathers

Other differences between fathers and mothers may be their concerns and priorities for their child and family. Several authors have reported that fathers express more concern than mothers about future issues such as the child's ability to be self-supporting, the cost of providing for the child, the social dependency of the child, and legal concerns (Meyer, Vadasy, Fewell, & Schell, 1982). Conversely, mothers may be more concerned about the day-to-day issues of their child such as friendships with other children or their child's nutritional needs. When mothers and fathers have different concerns, the issues of both parents should be priorities for service providers.

In a survey conducted by Bailey and Simeonsson (1988), mothers reported twice as many family needs for services and supports than did fathers. In another study (Flynn & Wilson, 2003), fathers and mothers individually ranked services and supports. Preliminary results indicate that mothers identified information about their child's disability and ways she can help her child as most important. On the other hand, fathers chose service-oriented functions such as involvement with early intervention and respite care as most important for  their child and family. Finally, in another study which utilized the "Survey of Family Needs" (Bailey & Simeonsson, 1988) researchers found that fathers expressed a greater need for help in locating a doctor while mothers indicated a greater need for more friends to talk to and more time for themselves (Allred & Cooper, 1991).

Since fathers and mothers may differ in their priorities, there may be increased difficulty in fulfilling so-called family goals as a result of the father not "buying into" the intervention efforts (Allred, 1992). An implication for service providers is that input from both parents may be essential, rather than "good when it happens." As a service provider, you might unintentionally send the message that the father's participation is nice, but services can be provided effectively without him.

Relationship Between Interventionists and Fathers

People often exhibit a higher level of comfort when discussing personal matters with an individual of the same gender. It can be observed that most EI/ECSE service providers are female. There is a level of comfort when women talk with other women and perhaps relate to one another as mothers. The same level of comfort may not be present when female service providers talk to and work with fathers. Conversely, fathers may experience less comfort when talking with service providers of the opposite sex. Fathers and service providers who have different cultural backgrounds may find communication even more challenging.

Think about your own level of comfort when talking to fathers versus mothers. Do you find yourself inadvertently seeking out mothers rather than fathers? For example, when you make a phone call to a family about their child, do you ask for the mother or father when another

family member answers the phone? If you are working in a center-based program and a child gets sick, do you tend to call the mother or father first? Our guess is that most service providers seek out the mother during these situations. One of the reasons might be because you have spent considerable time developing a relationship with the mother. If you are a female service provider, another reason could be because you are more comfortable talking with the mother.

Another gender difference between men and women is that females generally prefer relationship-building while males are more individualistic and competitive (Tannen, 1990). In EI/ECSE, fathers may want to discuss just the facts and the options for supports and services. On the other hand, mothers may desire and seek opportunities for sharing and listening. Fathers may view this approach as intrusive and not helpful to the family (Turbiville, Turnbull, & Turnbull, 1995). Fathers may view relationship-building as a secondary effect of their initial goal: securing services for their child. However, many current recommended practices in early intervention are premised on the relationship between the service provider and the family (Turbiville, Turnbull, Garland, & Lee, 1996). While relationships are important, the recognition that some fathers may want to talk and many others may want to do is also critical.

Ideas for the Interventionist

Service providers may need to evaluate and alter their own assumptions and practices to effectively include and support fathers. By evaluating your own beliefs and knowledge about fathers, and your skills, you may discover new insights and ways to enhance your practices in early intervention.

Recognize Your Own Beliefs and Perspectives

An initial step in becoming more competent with fathers is self-awareness. All of us have preconceived beliefs and values about the roles of fathers in raising children. As service providers, we may find ourselves unknowingly stereotyping individuals within the family, particularly with families who are culturally diverse. These potential biases are generally due to our upbringing and/or our experiences in life. For instance, some people may believe that fathers should assume a 50-50 role in the everyday care of his child. Others may think mothers should be the person to pack the lunch every morning and facilitate bathtime at night. Service providers who express personal biases may create barriers and actually prevent fathers from assuming a more active role in the services being provided. To better understand your interactions with fathers, consider the following ideas:

- Critically examine your values and viewpoints. What biases do you have that might interfere with your ability to facilitate a father's involvement?
- Understand your personal perspectives about the roles and expectations of fathers. How did experiences with your own father influence your beliefs about fathers today?
- Identify and acknowledge your level of comfort with fathers. Does talking to fathers make you more nervous than conversing with mothers?
- Recognize any cultural, racial, or linguistic biases which you might have.
- Spend some time reflecting on how you seek input from fathers as compared to mothers.
- Review your work-related activities over the past month. Compare the number of times you talked to mothers versus fathers.

... [F]athers may want to discuss just the facts and the options for supports and services. On the other hand, mothers may desire and seek opportunities for sharing and listening.

Think about your priorities when first meeting a child who is going to be enrolled in your program and his or her family. Do you value the importance of establishing relationships as a first priority? How are the conversations different when your first interaction is with the father rather than the mother? All of us have preferences which directly or indirectly guide our interactions with family members. We tend to consistently utilize and rely on those preferences and priorities.

By identifying your biases, beliefs, and preferences, you will be better able to adjust your personal communication style and interactions with and expectations of fathers. Personal reflection and self-awareness are the first steps in exploring how to expand EI/ECSE services to include and meet the needs of fathers.

Increase Your Knowledge and Skills

The next step is to increase your knowledge about fathers and your skills in working with them. Sparling, Biller, and Berger (1992) hypothesize that fathers may limit their involvement in their children's educational experience because professionals lack knowledge about fathers' interests, priorities, and concerns for their child. Involving fathers from the beginning, acknowledging their critical role, and identifying their priorities can facilitate a more active role for fathers. When fathers are not expected to play a primary role, a self-fulfilling prophecy may occur. Not only must service providers listen to the father's perspective and respect his choices, but also respond to his preferences.

Involving fathers from the beginning, acknowledging their critical role, and identifying their priorities can facilitate a more active role for fathers.

One way to more actively include fathers is to consider the type of activities that are chosen for intervention. Those activities may not be ones that interest a father or ones that are a part of his typical routine with his child. For instance, if intervention is chosen during naturally occurring events such as bathtime and the mother is the person in the family who typically has that role, the father may inadvertently be excluded. Most often, the routines and settings of mothers are considered by service providers and then often generalized to other family members, including the father (Turbiville et al., 1995). Thus, inadvertently, fathers' interests and personal stake may be marginalized, as well as his specific priorities and preferences for his children. By including fathers in the identification and selection of routines in which to base assessment and intervention, his investment and participation may increase.

Here are some ideas to become more knowledgeable about and skilled with fathers:

- Read articles and books about the influence of fathers on their child's development.

- Seek information about men's and women's differences in communication and interaction styles as well as differences in cultural practices.
- Learn to communicate with fathers and interpret both verbal and nonverbal communication such as eye contact, facial expressions, body language, gestures, and proximity.
- Spend a few afternoons in the park and observe fathers with their children. Notice how fathers talk to and interact with their children.
- Talk with your father, husband, brother, or other dads about their viewpoints on raising children. Ask them what their priorities are for their children.
- Talk with fathers honestly and openly. Make continued and sincere attempts to understand their points of view.
- Practice including fathers from the beginning. If fathers cannot participate in the first few sessions, do not give up. Continue to offer opportunities for involvement.

One of the best ways to enhance your skills in working with fathers in EI/ECSE is to spend time with them. Thus, one goal for service providers may be to facilitate opportunities for fathers' involvement. To reach this goal, flexibility is crucial. For example, a father's and mother's work schedules may be different. If both parents cannot be present at the same time during a session, you may want to alternate your schedule so that the mother can be involved with one visit and the father, the next. This might mean visiting a child in the morning one week and in the evening the next week. Also, make appointments and other scheduled events far enough in advance to allow fathers to include the event in their schedule.

Services and supports that are provided in contexts that enhance the participation of both parents will be most successful. This could include the time of day in which meetings, assessments, and services are scheduled; the type of activities conducted; and the location of services. Barriers that may exclude fathers should be identified, examined, and addressed in such a way as to deliver a strong message that the service provider values, seeks, and utilizes fathers' input and participation.

One of the best ways to enhance your skills in working with fathers in EI/ECSE is to spend time with them.

Given this information, caution is advised when making generalizations about individual family members who have unique ways of thinking and acting. By identifying the priorities, support needs, interaction styles, and work schedules of each father and mother, service providers can create opportunities for each parent to participate in vital decisions and everyday events. One of your greatest challenges may be to develop and maintain a satisfying, working relationship with both fathers and mothers. The responsibility falls not only on the shoulders of the service provider, but also on the EI/ECSE program.

Ideas for the EI/ECSE Program

Most programs providing services to young children have an advisory board, a governing board, or other decision-making committees. When we examine the policies and practices promoted in our current EI/ECSE programs, we need to ask ourselves if fathers are active participants on these boards and committees or if the family membership is comprised mostly of mothers. Program priorities and goals may be greatly influenced by the inclusion of fathers' perspectives.

Another strategy to facilitate more active participation of fathers is to make every effort to have male staff members. Men might be able to elicit special interests and concerns from fathers more easily than women.

As program administrators and staff, evaluate your organization's knowledge and competency in working effectively with fathers. Consider incorporating some of these additional strategies into your planning and implementation process:

- Conduct staff training on potential fathers' issues and those resulting from cultural diversity.
- Conduct staff training on techniques to enhance communication and interaction with fathers.
- Include fathers as presenters or panel members in training efforts to share their expertise or experiences.
- Show a videotape of fathers of children with disabilities at your next staff inservice training.
- Provide books and articles about fathers to staff and discuss their content.
- Personally invite fathers to participate in special events sponsored by your program.
- Develop a fathers' support group with active leadership from fathers.
- Review materials distributed by your program and ensure they are written in a manner likely to engage men as well as women.

- If a couple is physically separated or divorced, send all information to both parents, if legally appropriate. Do the same with stepfathers who are involved in raising the children.

The type of involvement which an EI/ECSE program offers may make a difference in the father's interest and willingness to participate. For example, a program might sponsor an afternoon in the park for fathers and their children or perhaps a trip to the zoo for dads and kids. If an afternoon of *activities* is organized rather than a verbal exchange, fathers may be more likely to want to be involved both with their children and with your program.

Conclusion

Ideas have been provided to help include fathers in the delivery of services and supports. We encourage you to think about each of the recommendations and reflect upon your own competencies as well as the practices and policies within your program. Just as with mothers, fathers will choose various levels of participation with their children and with EI/ECSE services. Service providers need to accept fathers at whatever level of involvement they choose and slowly build and encourage greater levels of participation in the process. Changing the "culture" of EI/ECSE services to include and meet the needs of both mothers and fathers is a shift in current thinking and practice. As we know, change often takes time. However, as service providers become more competent in interacting with fathers, the outcomes for children are likely to improve. Partnerships with fathers are an important component of family-centered services and supports.

Note
You can reach Linda Flynn-Wilson by e-mail at LFlynnWi@uno.edu

References
Allred, K. (1992). Fathers of young children with disabilities. *DEC Communicator, 18*(3), 6-7.
Allred, K., & Cooper, C. (1991). A comparison of mothers' versus fathers' needs for support in caring for a young child with special needs. Infant-Toddler Intervention: *The Transdisciplinary Journal, 2*(3), 205-221.
Bailey, D. B., & Simeonsson, R. J. (1988). Assessing needs of families with handicapped infants. *Journal of Special Education, 22*(1), 117-127.
Davis, P. B., & May, J. E. (1991). Involving fathers in early intervention and family support programs: Issues and strategies. *Children's Health Care, 20*(2), 87-91.
Easterbrooks, M. A., & Goldberg, W. A. (1984). Toddler development in the family: Impact of father involvement and parenting characteristics. *Child Development, 55*, 740-752.
Flynn, L. L., & Wilson, P. (2003). *Concerns and priorities: What families are saying*. Manuscript submitted for publication.
Frey, K. S., Fewell, R. R., & Vadasy, P. F. (1989). Parental adjustment and changes in child outcome among families of young handicapped children. *Topics in Early Childhood Special Education, 8*(4), 38-57.
Hornby, G. (1992). A review of fathers' accounts of their experiences of parenting children with disabilities. *Disabilities Handicap Society, 7*(4), 363-374.
Lamb, M. (1986). The changing roles of fathers. In M.C. Lamb (Ed.), *The father's role: Applied perspectives* (pp. 3-28). New York: Wiley.

Lamb, M. E., Pleck, J. H., Charnov, E. L., & Levine, J. A. (1987). A biosocial perspective on paternal behavior and treatment. In J. Lancaster, J. Altmann, A. Rossi, & L. Sherrod, (Eds.), *Parenting across the lifespan.* New York: Aldine DeGruyter.

Lambie, R., & Daniels-Mohring, D. (1993). *Family systems within educational contexts.* Denver, CO: Love Publishing.

McLinden, E. (1990). Mothers' and fathers' reports of the effects of a young child with special needs on the family. *Journal of Early Intervention, 14*(3), 249-259.

Meyer, D., Vadasy, P., Fewell, R., & Schell, G. (1982). Involving fathers of handicapped infants: Translating research into program goals. *Journal of the Division for Early Childhood, 5*, 64-72.

Parke, R. (1988). *Fathers.* Boston: Cambridge University Press.

Pruett, K. (1993). The paternal presence. *Family Society, 74*(1), 46-50.

Sparling, J., Biller, M., & Berger, R. (1992). Fathers: Myth, reality and Public Law 99-457. *Infants and Young Children, 4*(3), 9-19.

Tannen, D. (1990). *You just don't understand.* New York: Ballantine.

Turbiville, V. P., Turnbull, A. P., Garland, C. W., & Lee, I. M. (1996). Development and implementation of IFSPs and IEPs: Opportunities for empowerment. In S. Odom & M. McLean (Eds.), *Early intervention/Early childhood special education: Recommended practices.* Austin, TX: Pro-Ed.

Turbiville, V. P., Turnbull, A. P., & Turnbull, H. R. (1995). Fathers and family-centered early intervention. *Infants and Young Children, 7*(4), 12-19.

Writing Outcomes That Make a Difference for Children and Families

Sharon E. Rosenkoetter, Ph.D.,
Oregon State University

Sara Squires, Parent,
Families Together, Topeka, KS

The individualized family service plan (IFSP) is intended to: (1) guide the intervention strategies for infants, toddlers, and young children with special needs; as well as to (2) select the informal and formal services that will make a developmental difference for them; and (3) support their families in their parenting roles (Beckman, Robinson, Rosenberg, & Filer, 1994; McGonigel, Kauffmann, & Johnson, 1991). The IFSP is required by law (Individuals with Disabilities Education Act [IDEA] Amendments of 1997, Part C) for children from birth to age three and their families to receive early intervention services. The IFSP planning process may also be employed up to the child's sixth birthday if the state, the family, and the local service program agree to use it (IDEA, 1997, Part B).

The heart of the IFSP is the outcome statements, which define a planning team's shared vision for the child and its subsequent step-by-step plan for achieving that vision. Families, service coordinators, and other practitioners involved in the planning process spend a great deal of time and thought in writing outcome statements to guide the course of early intervention. Written and implemented well, these outcome statements map the path that team members will take together. Identification of suitable outcomes can make a real difference at a critical developmental time for infants, toddlers, and young children

> *The heart of the IFSP is the outcome statements ... [these] map the path that team members will take together.*

and their families (Carnegie Task Force on Meeting the Needs of Young Children, 1994; Rosin, Whitehead, Tuchman, Jesien, & Begun, 1993).

Wise planning for IFSP outcomes conforms to the law by addressing the people and places with whom young children and their families spend time (IDEA, 1997, Part C)—their so-called "natural environments." Well-considered IFSP outcomes build on the unique combination of resources, priorities, and concerns that each family brings to nurturing their young child with special needs (McGonigel, Woodruff, & Roszmann-Millican, 1994). In addition, meaningful outcomes target the anticipated knowledge, skills, and activities by adults and other children that will aid the young child in learning during the family's everyday activities (Bricker, Pretti-Frontczak, & McComas, 1998). Outcome statements should use each family's own language and must *not* use language that the family cannot understand (Kansas Department of Health and Environment, 1997; McGonigel, Kauffmann, & Johnson, 1991). Clearly, outcome statements that fit these criteria are very different from traditional, agency-oriented, therapeutically-worded goal statements.

Effective outcome statements are very much a work in progress: plan to change the IFSP at least several times per year as the infant or young child grows and as the family's preferences, resources, and challenges change. This article will describe one thinking process that can lead to meaningful outcomes for each child and family. Then it will offer questions for families and service providers to use to evaluate the outcome statements they craft together. Finally, it will provide a framework for thinking about outcomes to ensure that broad possibilities are considered and those with potentially the greatest impact on development are chosen.

Effective outcome statements are very much a work in progress ....

The outcome development process described here was created in collaboration with and to provide a framework for IFSP teams in one midwestern state. After initial training of practitioners, the process was implemented in locally appropriate ways by IFSP teams in both rural and urban areas. Flexibility in adoption was considered essential due to differing models for family service coordination, assessment, and service delivery in various parts of the state. Ongoing technical assistance was provided as requested. Copious anecdotal data support the statement that implementing this process has helped IFSP teams connect the IFSP with families' daily lives.

The Thinking Process

Perhaps even more important than the words written on paper for the IFSP is the process of exploration that the family and service providers experience together. The duration, complexity, and candor of this exploration will depend upon several factors: (1) the openness of participants to question and hear one another, (2) the time given to the process, and (3) the family's previous experience with service providers in general and with these particular early intervention providers in particular. Following is one way to approach the exploration.

The first step is to discuss: (1) the developmental priorities of family members and service providers for the child, (2) the concerns of the family about issues with any of their members that affect the child's development, and (3) their preferences for intervention emphasis during the next weeks and months. "Why this will make a difference to us and our child" should be understood by all before pen is put to paper to draft the IFSP.

The next step is to discuss the places where the child and family spend their time, along with the activities they do, or wish to do, in those places. The places mentioned may be outside the home (e.g., the locker room and pool for Mother-Tot Swim, the library story time, the cooperative play group), and/or they may be within the home (e.g., the floor of the family room, the highchair in the kitchen, the back yard play equipment). If professional members of the team have visited the settings that are important to the family, they can help the family plan developmentally meaningful interventions there.

Writing the actual outcome statement begins with the aim, stated as a proper noun and an observable, action verb; for example, "JunKoo will ride in an adapted seat on his mother's or father's bike during family bike trips ...."

The aim is followed by the rationale (e.g., "in order to ..."; "so that ..."; "to ..."). It tells why this action will make a difference for the family and child and underscores that everybody involved agrees on this rationale. Thus, any activity chosen is clearly linked to the team's aims for the child and family; for example, "... so that JunKoo can build balance and strength in his trunk muscles while enjoying an activity valued by his parents and brothers for family outings."

The persons writing the IFSP then list the steps that various people will take to achieve the outcome and when and where they will do them. The steps often will occur in the places that the family has previously described, with the people who typically spend time there. They often will address the developmental needs of the child or the desires of other family members to participate more fully and comfortably in their chosen activities. Note that if a therapeutic plan in technical language is needed for third-party payers, then the steps of that intervention can be appended to the IFSP document. It is important that the steps listed with the outcome statement are offered in nontechnical language.

The IFSP planners also decide how they will know if they have achieved their aim(s). This evaluation plan should be appropriate to the setting where it will occur. For example, if the child is learning to reach for an object, does she successfully locate and grab a cracker or a cookie of her own choice at lunch time? If the child is learning to make eye contact with others, does he do so when receiving his Happy Meal at McDonald's? Stated differently, the evaluation question should reflect " ... the importance of understanding the whole child, the child in context, and the complex interdependencies between learner and context that directly and indirectly influence what and how a child learns" (Salisbury & Vincent, 1990, p. 82). Phrase the evaluation of an outcome in terms meaningful to the family, rather than employing esoteric statistical data. Gathering data should be as unobtrusive as possible, perhaps evidenced in quickly jotted notes or recollections of informal observations (Hutinger, 1994).

> *The IFSP planners also decide how they will know if they have achieved their aim(s). This evaluation plan should be appropriate to the setting where it will occur.*

This thinking process as practiced in routine team discussions—and the attainment of some of the outcomes it formulates—will continue to lead to new priorities for family members and service providers as they update the IFSP in the future.

Questions to Evaluate Outcome Statements

In evaluating previously written outcomes or in creating new outcome statements, several questions are helpful because they revisit the thinking process described:

1. Do we know *why* we're writing this? Is this outcome *important* to this family's long-term aims for their child and their own family support agenda? Again, the purpose of the IFSP process is not to create a paper for the family's file, but rather to explore the team's shared aims and translate them into everyday actions that contribute incrementally to developmental growth.

2. Does this outcome mesh with activities that the family *chooses* to do? Is this outcome *do-able* within the family's daily routines and other current responsibilities and commitments? If the aim is important but the activities are impossible to implement given constraints on the family's resources, what *supports* can be provided to make it do-able? For example, JunKoo Kim's family would love to resume their previous schedule of family bike rides, but they will need consultation and ongoing support from a physical therapist and an equipment engineer to overcome the design challenge currently standing in the way of taking the toddler along.

3. Have we explored *informal*, *natural*, and *community-based* supports to determine whether they might accomplish developmental aims, rather than automatically listing more restrictive options? For example, a therapist might be able to work with a child and her playmates at her present child care center, rather than pulling her from that center to enroll her in a special program for children with disabilities. Answers to this question, of course, must be individually appropriate to the child and family. The whole team must determine them together.

4. Who will *pay* or *provide*? Will it be an agency within the community, the family, or a presently unknown entity? What programmatic actions are needed to locate funding and enlist commitment? Must specific language be used in the description of need to ensure that the desired payor will agree? Along with the family, early interventionists must become resource detectives, learning whom to contact to locate specialists for particular needs and find previously untapped financial resources. A number of states have hired personnel in their Part C programs to assist in resource finding. State developmental disabilities groups may be helpful. One parent and her family service coordinator spent a total of 30 hours on the World Wide Web, communicating with other parents of children with her child's condition and learning how other teams had put together multi-agency support for an expensive piece of assistive technology. Libraries, including medical school media centers, can also be helpful in locating sources of funding for special projects or services.

5. Is the outcome written in language the *family* might use, rather than in professional jargon?

6. Does this outcome really *matter* to this child and family? *Who* will benefit from this outcome? *Who* wants it? For example, one parent requested an IFSP-initiated training of church nursery workers to

enable her child to enjoy a new social opportunity, the child's twin to avoid continually translating for her sister, and the family to participate in church activities without worrying about their daughter's safety or happiness.

Observation of numerous IFSPs by the authors indicates that early intervention personnel and family/service provider teams often draft outcomes before they observe families' natural environments. Such teams can get into a rut by repeatedly writing the same types of outcomes for the various children whom they serve. Unfortunately, when written outcomes are too limited, young children's learning and their families' commitment to the IFSP process may also be restricted.

Some Types of Outcomes That *Do* Make a Difference

Following are some familiar types of outcomes as well as some that you may not have considered. The framework is adapted from *Considering Child-Based Results for Young Children* (Kagan, Rosenkoetter, & Cohen, 1997).

Child Outcomes Focused on the Child in Daily Activities

Child Development Outcomes

These are achievements across the five developmental domains that are important for the family's or child's life now or prerequisite to critical future development. Example: "Tallie will move five steps with her walker toward another child in order to play more with other children in the play group."

Child Experience Outcomes

These relate to participation in activities that the child should encounter to prepare for future environments. Example: "Jared will attend weekly 'Mothers' Morning Out' in order to practice separating from his mom before starting preschool next fall."

Child Motivation Outcomes

These are actions that will enhance the child's enjoyment, desire to learn and participate, or engagement, all essential foundations for future learning. Example: "Inez will trigger at least four switches hooked to different action toys in her home in order to entertain herself for at least five minutes, both to have fun by herself and also to begin to put actions together to get what she wants."

Family Outcomes Focused on One or More Members of the Family in Activities That Influence Child Development

Family Information/Resource Finding Outcomes

These relate to family members or service providers securing information so that family members can make decisions about issues that matter to them, access desired resources, or make plans for the future. Example: "Marcella will work with the physical therapist to learn about the effect of spastic quadriplegia such as Willa's during childhood and later in adult-hood, so that Marcella can anticipate her daughter's challenges and plan for their family's future needs."

Family Finance Outcomes

This is the gathering of information to aid the family in its financial planning. Example: "Lee and Chang will work with their family service coordinator in order to gain information about SSI so they can deter-mine whether SSI money might be available to help them with Tiuu."

Family Social-Emotional Support Outcomes

These are actions to assist the family in locating and building friendships and other supportive associations. Examples: "With help from her fam-ily service coordinator, Jody will find, train, and use babysitters so that she can participate in the Bible study and prayer group at St. Patrick's Church for her personal well-being," or, "With help from Families Together, Stephanie and Jon will network with other couples in the Parent to Parent Network who have preschool-aged children with Down Syndrome, in order to make new friends who can understand their daily life."

Family Enhancement Outcomes

These relate to accomplishing actions to improve the family's health, safety, and quality of life. Example: "Margaret and her family service coordinator will work together to move Margaret and the children into safer, more affordable housing in order to reduce their risk of violence and ease Margaret's worries about safety."

Family Personal Outcomes

This is the achievement of actions to increase a family's capacity to parent their child(ren). Example: "With help from his family service coordinator,

Enrique will find a language tutor and enroll in the alternate high school degree program so that he can get a better job to support his family as he wishes."

Network and Infrastructure Outcomes Focused on Actions by One or More Agencies in the Service Network/State Administrative Structure That Supports Early Intervention

Further Assessment Outcomes

These are system actions to gather more information to aid in planning for the child or family. Example: "Ellie and Paul will work with their family service coordinator, community agencies, and funders to get more extensive audiological testing for Jason in order to better plan for his language activities."

Acquisition of Equipment or Materials Outcomes

These relate to an analysis of child and family contexts, the ordering of needed items, acquiring them, and training all relevant people to use them. Examples: "With help from Easter Seals, Paula and Pete will obtain a wheelchair appropriate for Megan, and they will learn how to use it, in order to be able to take Megan more places that the family wishes to go," or, "With help from (a community agency for adults with special needs), Paula (who has a physical impairment) will obtain and learn to use a special changing table so that she can change Larisa's diapers."

Personnel Outcomes

These are the early intervention system's responses to identified needs for additional or differently prepared personnel to support the family. Example: "With help from their family service coordinator and the East Asian Resource Committee, Mr. and Mrs. Ngyuen will find an interpreter who speaks Hmong and English to accompany the family to physician appointments so that the doctors and the Ngyuens can communicate about Bao's progress."

Location and Coordination of Needed Services Outcomes

These relate to finding needed services and fitting them together to create a single, unified program to support the family and child. Example: "Jake and the family service coordinator will work together with the Part C program and (two local school districts) to arrange for intervention services at a child care center near Jake's job (which is in an adjacent school district) in order for Jake to participate in Billy's therapy during his lunch hour."

Payment for Needed Services Outcomes

These relate to arranging funding for needed services. Example: "Martha and her family service coordinator will work with SRS and/or the local interchurch council to find funds for child care for Robbie so that Martha can return to work part-time."

Transportation Outcomes

These relate to arranging transportation needed by the family to support their child. Example: "With assistance from the family service coordinator and the women's group at Morningside Baptist Church, the Gomezes will arrange travel for themselves and child care for their other children so that they can regularly visit their baby in the NICU."

Training Outcomes

This is training and technical assistance needed by family members or agency staff to enable the child to be cared for safely and nurtured effectively. Example: "Four staff members at the child care center will be trained in and then demonstrate skills to operate the oxygen equipment, in order to allow Todd to participate fully and safely in center activities after he transitions to attending preschool there."

Summary

Early interventionists need to evaluate the outcomes they write with families and, with the assistance of families, modify the content and language if their outcomes are found wanting. A good way to do this is to work with a hypothetical or real case study, with outcome development and critique by multiple team members, including families. The questions to evaluate outcome statements that were provided in this article may be helpful in this analysis process.

Note also that issues that arise in developing network/infrastructure outcomes are worth sharing with agency and state administrators as well as with local inter-agency coordinating councils to guide future staff development and resource planning. Examples include multicultural sensitivities, equipment management, transition barriers, and funding challenges.

Notes

The concepts in this article were developed as part of technical assistance to early interventionists, in collaboration with Kansas Infant-Toddler Services, Kansas Department of Health and Environment. Most of this work was completed while Sharon Rosenkoetter was at the Associated Colleges of Central Kansas. You can reach Sharon E. Rosenkoetter by e-mail at sharon.rosenkoetteer@orst.edu

References

Beckman, P. J., Robinson, C. C., Rosenberg, S., & Filer, J. (1994). Family involvement in early intervention: The evolution of family-centered service. In L. J. Johnson, R. J. Gallagher, M. J. LaMontagne, J. B. Jordan, J. J. Gallagher, P. L. Hutinger, & M. B. Karnes (Eds.), *Meeting early intervention challenges: Issues from birth to three* (pp. 13-32). Baltimore: Paul H. Brookes.

Bricker, D., Pretti-Frontczak, K., & McComas, N. (1998). *An activity-based approach to early intervention.* Baltimore: Paul H. Brookes.

Carnegie Task Force on Meeting the Needs of Young Children. (1994). *Starting points: Meeting the needs of our youngest children.* New York: Carnegie Corp.

Hutinger, P. L. (1994). Linking screening, identification, and assessment with curriculum. In L. J. Johnson, R. J. Gallagher, M. J. LaMontagne, J. B. Jordan, J. J. Gallagher, P. L. Hutinger, & M. B. Karnes (Eds.), *Meeting early intervention challenges: Issues from birth to three* (pp. 51-94). Baltimore: Paul H. Brookes.

Individuals with Disabilities Education Act (IDEA) Amendments of 1997. (1997). 20 U.S.C., Secs. 1400-1485.

Kagan, S. L., Rosenkoetter, S., & Cohen, N. (1997). *Considering child-based results for young children: Definitions, desirability, feasibility, and next steps* (Report on issues forums conducted for the W. K. Kellogg Foundation, the Carnegie Corporation of New York, and Quality 2000). New Haven, CT: Yale Bush Center on Child Development and Social Policy.

Kansas Department of Health and Environment (KDHE). (1997). *Procedure manual for infant-toddler services in Kansas.* Topeka, KS: Author.

McGonigel, M. J., Kauffmann, R. K., & Johnson, B. H. (Eds.). (1991). *Guidelines and recommended practices for the individualized family service plan* (2nd ed.). Bethesda, MD: National Early Childhood Technical Assistance System and Association for the Care of Children's Health.

McGonigel, M. J., Woodruff, G., & Roszmann-Millican, M. (1994). The transdisciplinary team: A model for family-centered early intervention. In L. J. Johnson, R. J. Gallagher, M. J. LaMontagne, J. B. Jordan, J. J. Gallagher, P. L. Hutinger, & M. B. Karnes (Eds.), *Meeting early intervention challenges: Issues from birth to three* (pp. 95-132). Baltimore: Paul H. Brookes.

Rosin, P., Whitehead, A., Tuchman, L., Jesien, G., & Begun, A. (1993). *Partnerships in early intervention: A training guide on family-centered care, team building, and service coordination.* Madison, WI: University of Wisconsin, Waisman Center Early Intervention Program.

Salisbury, C. L., & Vincent, L. J. (1990). Criterion of the next environment and best practices: Mainstreaming and integration ten years later. *Topics in Early Childhood Special Education, 2,* 78-89.

Family-Centered Intervention:

Bridging the Gap Between IFSPs and Implementation

Lee Ann Jung, Ph.D., University of Kentucky
Caroline Gomez, Ph.D., Auburn University, Auburn, AL
Samera Baird, Ph.D., Auburn University, Auburn, AL

Amy is an early childhood special educator providing home-based services to 20 children in a rural community. She learned in college the importance of involving families in intervention, but now that she is in the "real world" she is realizing how difficult this can be. On her last home visit, Amy sat on the floor with Jared while his mother, Trisha, sat on the couch. She asked Trisha if she had been able to do any of the activities she suggested last week. Trisha said, "A few times. It's been a real crazy week getting his sister ready for school." Amy began working with Jared on communication, describing to Trisha what she was doing. Amy hoped Jared's mother would learn from her model and be able to work with Jared this week.

Like Amy, many professionals in early intervention may learn that for intervention to be successful, families and other caregivers must "follow through." Despite the importance of family involvement, very few professionals receive training on how to partner with families or how to teach caregivers (Washington, Schwartz, & Swinth, 1994). Consequently, when students graduate and begin working as early intervention professionals, many provide hands-on, child-focused, professionally-designed intervention without active family involvement (Harbin et al., 1998; Jung & Baird, 2003; McBride & Peterson, 1997). Professionals commonly attribute follow-through problems to families, indicating that families do not understand how important follow-through is, can't learn how to do the interventions, or do not care (Bernheimer & Keogh, 1995). However, the early intervention professional often fails to attribute the problem to the intervention design.

IFSP Outcomes Are Not Enough

The individualized family service plan (IFSP) is not intended to be a place to delineate the minuscule details of instructional design and intervention strategies. Rather, the IFSP is a vehicle for parents and professionals to partner together to select targeted outcomes that are meaningful to the family, and to develop a framework for achieving outcomes (Blasco, 2001). After a routines-based assessment has been completed and outcomes are chosen, intervention planning within the context of the natural environment can begin. An intervention plan is needed to move from the framework of the IFSP to specific procedures for intervention (Bricker, Pretti-Frontczak, & McComas, 1998) implemented by the family. An intervention plan is a systematic design for achieving a desired outcome. Intervention plans should include: (1) a long-term goal; (2) a short-term objective; (3) empirically based methods for achieving the short-term objective; and (4) a data collection system.

Intervention planning traditionally has focused on developing strategies for teaching a child specific, discrete skills that have been pulled directly from assessment instruments (Harbin et al., 1998). Current recommended practices from the Division for Early Childhood (DEC) of the Council for Exceptional Children (CEC) suggests that intervention targets should be focused on teaching skills that are necessary for children to function more completely and competently in their natural environments (Wolery, 2000). Further, these recommended practices state that the intervention targets should be based on the child's current behavior and abilities within the context of daily routines and on the family's views of what the child needs to learn rather than on the child's diagnostic classification. Tying the identification of outcomes for a child to the demands, expectations, and requirements of the child's current environments must take place in order to support each family's ability to implement intervention plans. Even when professionals use family-friendly language, if they use home visits for telling families what their child needs to learn and providing direct services, they send the message to families, "I am the expert. Your child gets better intervention or therapy when I do it."

Families have reported that when they have a simple, written plan they remember to use learning opportunities in ways they discussed with professionals (Dunst, Bruder, Trivette, Raab, & McLean, 2001). Furthermore, an intervention plan may be empowering to families and other caregivers because the plan explicitly delineates instructional procedures and demonstrates confidence in and reliance on their ability to implement the intervention. Thus, the purpose of this article is to describe a method for developing written intervention plans that can be used with families to assist in bridging the gap between the outcomes targeted on the IFSP and the interventions planned for implementation in natural environments. Though identification of family-focused outcomes is essential to the IFSP process, this is not the focus of this article. Rather, the focus is on refining the child-focused outcomes from IFSPs, and developing plans to address these outcomes within the context of families' daily experiences.

Developing and Implementing Child-Focused Intervention Plans

The intervention planning process described in this article was developed to facilitate the design of child-focused interventions to be implemented by families and caregivers. The intervention planning process involves the following seven steps: (1) refining IFSP outcomes for intervention, (2) analyzing baseline functional behavior, (3) identifying natural learning opportunities, (4) selecting empirically supported strategies, (5) ensuring fidelity, (6) developing a data collection system, and (7) evaluating the plan. Table 1 (see following page) provides a brief checklist with criteria for the early interventionist to use to assess the fidelity of implementation of each step of the process. The Appendix includes a sample written intervention plan in which the planning process has been applied. This sample plan is used to illustrate the seven-step process as each step is described.

Step One: Refining IFSP Outcomes for Intervention

Child-focused outcomes that appear on the IFSP typically are predicted to be achievable within six months to coincide with the six-month review date. Therefore, IFSP child-focused outcomes are often appropriate as long-term goals when designing intervention plans. In the example plan for Maisie (see Appendix), the IFSP outcome, "Maisie will walk without help and without falling" translated well into the long-term goal for her intervention plan.

Table 1: Checklist for Intervention Plan Development

Step	Criteria	✓
One: Refining IFSP Outcomes	Is the outcome likely to be achieved within two to four months?	
	Is the outcome necessary for development or for better functioning?	
	Is the outcome clearly related to a family priority or concern?	
	Does the outcome include rationale, circumstances, and criteria?	
Two: Baseline Behavior Analysis	Has the team discussed with the family the child's behavior as well as antecedents and consequences of demonstration of the behavior?	
	Have team members observed the child's behavior relative to the objective for an understanding of his or her current abilities?	
Three: Identifying Natural Learning Opportunities	Has a routines-based or similar assessment been conducted?	
	Has the team identified settings, activities, and routines in which learning could occur?	
	Has the team identified settings, activities, and routines in which intervention would be difficult to implement and should therefore be excluded?	
Four: Selecting Strategies	Have developmentally enhancing techniques that the family is already using been identified and included in the intervention plan?	
	Have empirically based intervention strategies been selected that will support the achievement of the objective?	
	Do the selected intervention strategies clearly indicate the family's role as implementer?	
Five: Ensuring Fidelity of Intervention	Has the plan been clearly and thoroughly explained to all team members using clear, concrete examples?	
	Has the intervention been clearly demonstrated for implementer(s)?	
	Did the implementer(s) have an opportunity to demonstrate the intervention?	
	Did the implementer(s) receive feedback and suggestions if needed?	
	Did those team members observing the implementer(s) convey confidence in the implementer(s)' ability to use the new strategy?	
Six: Developing a Data Collection System	Is the system understandable and an appropriate match for the family's routines?	
	Does the data collection method match the objective?	
	Does the system allow for ease of data collection by the family (formally or informally)?	
	Does the system include a method to graph progress?	
Seven: Evaluating the Plan	Did interventionists ask the family to share their evaluation of the child's progress?	
	Did interventionists review data with the family?	
	Did interventionists and family make modifications as needed?	

Once the long-term goal has been identified and agreed upon by all, the family and professionals then break down this goal into short-term objectives. Development of a short-term objective should include four components: describing a rationale for the objective, defining the target behavior, identifying the circumstances, and determining the criteria for success. For Maisie the short-term objective developed for initial intervention toward achieving the long-term goal was, "Maisie will step over the thresholds in her house with-

out help or falling each time she tries for one week so she can move between rooms safely and independently."

Describing a Rationale for the Objective

The rationale for the objective should demonstrate the relevance of the objective to the child and family's life. A functional outcome is one that is either necessary for child development or for better functioning of the child or family in the natural environment (Bailey & Wolery, 1992). In the example for Maisie, the rationale is, "so she can move between rooms safely and independently." When families select outcomes based on their child's functioning in daily routines, the child-focused outcomes on the IFSP should already be functional and tied to a specific family concern or priority. Nonetheless, professionals may need to review these associated priorities and concerns to ensure current relevance.

Defining the Target Behavior

The target behavior for short-term objectives selected for an intervention plan should be an action verb that is observable, measurable, repeatable, and has the potential to be achieved within two to four months. Setting small, reachable behavior goals will allow the intervention to be designed in a way that addresses each specific step toward the IFSP outcome. For some children progress occurs slowly, and caregivers can become discouraged. When intervention plans are designed to detect small changes, even small increments of progress will be evident and can be celebrated.

Identifying the Circumstances

Identifying the circumstances involves determining under what conditions the child is likely to need the target behavior. Through this process interventionists and families make explicit connections between the target behavior and circumstances in which it is needed. By identifying circumstances with families, the developmental outcome is contextualized in an individualized description of how this particular child will use this behavior or skill in his or her day-to-day activities. As strategies to support the identified outcome are discussed with families, interventionists can refer to the circumstances to tailor the explanation of the strategy. For Maisie, who was ready to develop her skills in walking, this means instead of discussing with the family generic ways to improve Maisie's ability to walk on uneven surfaces, for example, the interventionists would discuss specific ways to help Maisie learn to step over the thresholds in her house. Specifying circumstances also serves to make the objective more measurable by giving all team members an understanding of exactly when the child is expected to display the behavior or use the skill. For Maisie, this means everyone will be focusing on this skill when she goes between rooms in her house.

When intervention plans are designed to detect small changes, even small increments of progress will be evident and can be celebrated.

Determining the Criteria for Success

By including criteria for success, the family and professionals know exactly what the desired outcome is and will be able to measure when the objective is met. Because families will be identifying progress toward the outcome, criteria should be sufficiently specific without being complicated. An example of a complicated criterion is, "7 out of 10 trials for 5 consecutive data collection days." This criterion, though very specific and in line with recommended practices for writing behavioral objectives, may not be family-friendly because it insinuates that the family must concentrate on collecting formal data ten times per day, which transforms what should be a natural routine into data collection sessions. Second, this criterion could be disempowering to some families in that it includes language that is likely unfamiliar and possibly intimidating. A more appropriate criterion is, "… at every meal time each day or until the family is satisfied with progress." From Maisie's plan, the criterion is "without help and without falling each time she tries for a week."

Step Two: Baseline Functional Analysis of Behavior

In order to develop strategies and measure progress, professionals and families need to talk about the child's current behavior or development related to the short-term objective. Team members can design an intervention that is more likely to be effective if they have an understanding of the child's current behaviors relative to the objective, what usually precedes the various behaviors (i.e., antecedents), and what usually occurs immediately following the behavior (i.e., consequences). Some of this discussion should have occurred as a part of choosing the short-term objective. Professionals can gain information on baseline behavior by observing the child in the natural environment and by asking caregivers to provide information. Maisie's team learned through observation that she was able to cross the threshold with help and attempted to cross it frequently. The team members needed to know more about Maisie's behavior and through discussion with the family learned that Maisie really enjoys meal times and is most likely to walk across the threshold at these times. The questions found in Table 2 are examples of those that team members might use to facilitate this type of conversation with families about baseline behavior. The resulting information not only helps professionals explain empirically based strategies to families in the context of the situation, but also allows team members to measure progress. To determine if the intervention is in fact working, there must be an understanding of the child's ability or behavior before the intervention began.

Table 2: Questions to Facilitate Baseline Functional Analysis of Behavior

Question Categories	Sample Questions for Walking
What does the child do now?	How does she choose to get around most of the time?
	Can she walk holding on to furniture without falling?
What can the child do with help?	Does she ask for help when she wants to walk?
	How much help does she need to walk?
	What kind of help does she need?
When does the behavior occur?	When does she enjoy walking?
	Under what conditions does she walk best?
What are the child's interests?	What are her favorite things to do that include walking?
	What are some things that make her happy or excited?

Step Three: Identifying Natural Learning Opportunities

Professionals can make families feel like they need to sacrifice their normal lives to work on their child's development. Traditional, skill-oriented intervention suggestions left by professionals may be translated by caregivers to mean, "If I care about my child I must do these things," which can lead to a family either disrupting their normal life to provide intervention divorced from everyday routines or feeling guilty that they are not. Based on a longitudinal study, Bernheimer and Keogh (1995) proposed that the disparity between a professional's good advice and the practice of the family could often be attributed to a mismatch between

the professional's intervention plans and the family's everyday routines.

Routines by definition are activities that occur regularly and repeatedly (Bricker & Cripe, 1992; Prizant & Bailey, 1992). By asking the family to choose the routines in which to embed intervention, routines are then " ... functional and predictable activities that match the interests and individual schedules of the child and family" (Cripe & Venn, 1997, p. 20). These routines then provide for many brief teachable moments throughout the day (Cripe & Venn, 1997; Rule, Losardo, Dinnebeil, Kaiser, & Rowland, 1998). The service provider should suggest strategies that are easily incorporated within the natural routines of the family and provide an example of a family routine or activity using the strategy. For example, during bath time a caregiver might say the word "bubbles" when touching bubbles in the bath. The service provider could explain that using this strategy during every bath may increase the likelihood of the child making the connection between the word and the bubbles.

Prior to IFSP development, a service provider should already have completed a routines-based (McWilliam, 1992) or similar assessment, such as the "Ecological Congruence Assessment" (Wolery, Brashers, & Neitzel, 2002). As the professional and family plan intervention strategies, they should review the family's daily routines and activities and consider within which routines or activities each objective might fit. Also important is consideration of the child's interests and motivators that emerged from the baseline analysis of behavior to delineate some possible opportunities for incidental intervention. For example, through this process Maisie's interventionists learned that she is most likely to want to move from room to room during meal times. A routines-based interview can also help identify any circumstances that may preclude the inclusion of intervention into a routine. For example, a child's mother may say something like, "Dinner is really the only time I talk with my husband. I'd rather not be distracted by having to concentrate on my child's labeling objects at that time."

As the professional and family plan intervention strategies, they should review the family's daily routines and activities and consider within which routines or activities each objective might fit.

Step Four: Selecting Strategies to Facilitate Learning

In selecting techniques to facilitate learning, a service provider should: (1) identify developmentally enhancing techniques families are already using, and (2) assist the family in selecting empirically based strategies to maximize their child's learning.

Identify Techniques the Family Is Using

Most parents spontaneously engage in some caregiving techniques that are consistent with optimal infant development. Examples include using "motherese," and interpreting and quickly responding to infant behaviors. Before discussing new intervention strategies, a service provider should identify the positive techniques caregivers are already using. Providing the family with a list of example routines (see Dunst, Herter, Shields, & Bennis, 2001) can help initiate conversations about natural learning opportunities. For Maisie, team members might have noticed that the family praised Maisie for trying to cross a threshold. The team could then talk to the family about how this praise is an effective strategy they are using and ways that it can be used in the intervention plan.

Families can then identify additional settings or opportunities specific to them (Tisot & Thurman, 2002). Everyday things that families do with their children (e.g., caring for pets, reading stories, grocery shopping) can be rich experiences for enhancing development. Many people such as neighbors, extended family, and family friends have opportunities to address a child's outcomes and may be included in intervention planning. Siblings are often important play partners for the child and may instinctively provide intervention for years to come (Schwartz & Rodriguez, 2001).

Selecting Empirically-Based Strategies to Maximize Learning

Once contexts for addressing outcomes are chosen, teams can discuss strategies that are likely to be developmentally enhancing. According to DEC recommended practices, "A strategy is an organized procedure for guiding adults' behavior in interacting with, and promoting the learning of young children with disabilities"(Wolery, 2000, p. 32). Service providers should be knowledgeable of intervention methods and current research on effective practices in order to be able to select strategies with families.

When discussing strategies to address desired outcomes with families, the service provider should use lay terms. For example, it is unlikely that a family would be familiar with the term "labeling" in a learning context. Instead, the service provider should explain that a good strategy for teaching their child words is "talking about what the child sees." For Maisie, the team began by talking about environmental modifications needed to help her succeed. In her plan, only the minor modification of keeping the doorways clutter-free was needed. The intervention strategy selected for Maisie was "system of least prompts," though the label was not used to describe the strategy in the intervention plan. Her family was taught the strategy through a series of "if-then" statements. For example, if Maisie begins to fall, the family knows to give her physical assistance to intercept the fall and help her over the threshold. The team members talked with her family about how to help Maisie generalize this skill to other times when she needs to be able to step over objects or move on uneven surfaces.

Step Five: Ensuring Fidelity of Intervention

Ensuring the fidelity or procedural consistency of empirically based intervention can also be challenging for service providers. Families may believe they understand how to use a particular strategy and yet implement the technique in a way that is inconsistent with the design. Providing concrete examples and modeling the strategy can increase the likelihood that caregivers will be comfortable using a strategy (McWilliam, 2000) thus increasing the probability of fidelity of intervention. Furthermore, by watching the family member use the strategy in a natural routine, the interventionist can assure the caregiver that he or she is likely to be effective in achieving the desired outcomes.

For example, if an intervention outcome is for a child to pull down his or her pants during toileting and a "Wait, Ask, Say, Show, and Do (WASSD)" strategy (McGee, Morrier, & Daly, 1999) is selected to address the outcome, the service provider can: (1) provide concrete examples of how this outcome could be addressed using the strategy, (2) model use of the selected strategy, and (3) offer to watch the family member as he or she uses the selected strategy.

Observation of the caregiver by the service provider can provide added assurance of fidelity of the intervention strategy. The role of the service provider is to offer suggestions to caregivers as they become proficient in using strategies. The service provider and caregiver can discuss ways to adapt the strategies in ways that are comfortable for the family and still similar to the empirically supported strategy. Once a strategy is chosen, the service provider's role is to convey to the caregivers confidence in their ability to provide intervention using the strategy.

Observation of caregivers' implementation of a strategy is not always necessary. Descriptive conversations may be as effective in some situations or more comfortable for a family. Even in instances where observation will likely be helpful to ensure fidelity, service providers should not pressure caregivers to try a strategy. Service providers should be perceptive to families' comfort level in demonstrating strategies. The rapport that will likely result from respecting a caregiver's choice not to demonstrate a strategy is more important than observing the strategy.

Step Six: Developing a Data Collection System

Teaching caregivers how to use specific intervention strategies is not sufficient to ensure fidelity of intervention. Data collection is an ongoing responsibility of the service provider and becomes challenging since most intervention takes place during the times the service provider is not present. However, data-based assessment is needed to determine the impact of the intervention on child progress and to make revisions in the intervention plan if necessary (Wolery, 2000). Without this critical feedback regarding the impact of intervention, valuable time may be lost and the needs of families may never fully be met (Gargiulo & Kilgo, 2000).

Teaching caregivers how to use specific intervention strategies is not sufficient to ensure fidelity of intervention. Data collection is an ongoing responsibility of the service provider ....

Data collection can be difficult, but the service provider can develop ways of tailoring data collection and record keeping for each family to prevent the process from becoming stressful. The service provider can offer families a variety of options for monitoring their child's progress (e.g., recording simple frequency, jotting down notes, remembering and sharing). For example, an observation checklist makes it possible to obtain a great deal of information in a relatively short period of time. When placed where the routine or activity takes place (e.g., bathroom mirror, refrigerator) with a pencil attached, the observation checklist can be an easy system that makes sense for families (Noonan & McCormick, 1993). Checklists can be as simple as a note with key words and dates. For Maisie, the interventionist designed a checklist to be left in the kitchen, which is where the family spends most of their time and is a location from which all the thresholds can be seen. The family member who sees Maisie go from one room to the next can simply mark the observation sheet with the appropriate letter depending on the level of assistance she needs to get across. When the interventionists next visit, they can discuss her progress since last time. The interventionists may want to plot the data on a graph for the family. A system for graphing data can provide an effective means to visually analyze the child's progress.

Formal written data collection systems are not always necessary or even appropriate. Some families will not want to collect formal data. Service providers need to be able to identify situations when formal data collection may be a burden to a family. In many instances data collection can be achieved through weekly conversations with the family. Notice with Maisie's intervention plan that although the intervention should be implemented each time she needs to go from room to room, the family has only been asked to record written data at meal times. This gives everyone a good idea of how Maisie is progressing without turning the entire day into a data session. Interventionists can ask families specific questions that will allow tracking of the data. Clearly, there are a variety of methods interventionists and families may choose to collect data. This is a vital part of the intervention planning process. The data should be used by interventionists to facilitate conversations with families about their child's progress and subsequent evaluation and revision to the intervention plan.

Step Seven: Evaluating the Plan

Information from the caregiver is essential when determining a child's progress towards an objective. Caregivers should be invited to speak first when sharing observations concerning their child's progress. According to Bailey (2003), "Maintaining an accepting attitude is important; judgmental comments, too much suggestion giving, and preaching are sure ways to cut a communicative interchange short" (p. 185). Attempting to find a balance between building independence in caregivers and offering support requires service providers to be perceptive and flexible in their interactions with caregivers.

Reviewing data with caregivers should assist in determining whether to modify the existing intervention plan. In some instances, slow progress warrants modifying the intervention plan. Caregiver concerns and priorities can also change over time, thereby making change in the intervention plan necessary. For example, a caregiver may initially feel insecure during interactions with a service provider. However, after experience with early intervention services and frequent interactions with the service provider, the care-

giver may feel more confident in his or her own opinions and skills and want to exert additional influence in intervention outcome selection (Bailey, 2003).

When modification or change is needed, the collaborative process begins once again with discussion of any changes in family and child routines as well as whether or not each of the previous outcomes is still considered important to the family. The service provider's role in this collaborative process is to provide support while assisting families as they make responsible and informed decisions concerning the intervention plan. When reflecting on early intervention services provided to her family, the mother of a toddler with Down syndrome stated, "Because the professionals in our lives looked at what we could do, when and where we could do it best, and then showed us how to do it ourselves, working on JP's skills has become a natural part of our lives" (Mullis, 2002, p. 24). Should not this parent's experience be every service provider's goal in providing early intervention services to families?

Conclusion

Implementing recommended practices, though necessary, is not sufficient. The goal of early intervention is to minimize the impact of developmental delay or disability on children and families. Professionals must ensure that the practices they employ and teach families to employ are indeed effective in progressing toward this goal. An intervention plan can assist professionals in refining IFSP objectives and developing effective and efficient procedures with caregivers, empowering families to maximize natural learning opportunities, and documenting efficacy and accountability.

Appendix

INTERVENTION PLAN FOR MAISIE

Parent/Caregiver ■ Planner ◻ Both ◧

Chronological Age 24 mos.
Developmental Age
Motor: 12-13 mos.
Cognitive: 18-20 mos.
Communication: 22-24 mos.

Short-Term Objective: Maisie will step over the thresholds in her house without help or falling each time she tries for one week so she can go between rooms safely and independently.

Intervention Planner: Samera   **Implementer(s):** Chris & Lee Ann

Family
Family wants Maisie to be able to walk independently so she doesn't get hurt and so they can more easily do things as a family.

Long-Term Goal
Maisie will walk without help and without falling.

Baseline Analysis
Date: 10/2/97
Did do: Maisie attempted to cross a threshold in her house and tripped.
Did not do: Cross the threshold without help or falling.

Natural Learning Opportunities
Routines: meal time, outside play time, bath time, bed time.
Incidental: Any time she needs to go to a new room at home.

Strategies to Facilitate Learning

Environmental Modifications: Keep **door areas free from toys or other objects** that could make crossing more difficult.

Incidental Instruction:
If Maisie steps over the threshold in the doorway without help and without falling, she gets to the other room quickly, and gains confidence in her abilities. **Clap and praise her.**

If Maisie approaches the threshold and does not appear to prepare to cross, **remind her by saying, "Step step, Maisie." Praise her as she crosses.**

If Maisie begins to fall as she crosses, attempt **to interept the fall and give her physical support to cross and praise for crossing.**

Generalization Procedures: Intervention strategies should be used any time Maisie needs or wants to walk from one room to another in her house.

Progress Record

Date:	Level of assistance given at meal times			Times with no help
	Breakfast	Lunch	Dinner	
10/8	P	P	V	0
10/13	P	P	V	0
10/20	V	V	V	0
10/22	V	I	V	1
10/29	P	I	I	1
11/3	I	V	I	2
11/5	I	I	V	2
11/10	V	I	V	1
11/17	I	V	I	2
11/19	I	I	I	3
12/3	I	I	I	3
12/4	I	I	I	3
12/5	I	I	I	3
12/6	I	I	I	3
12/7	I	I	I	3
12/8	I	I	I	3
12/9	I	I	I	3 Criteria Met

Legend
I = Independently
V = Verbal reminder that she is approaching door
P = Physical assistance to intercept a fall, help over threshold

Appendix: Intervention Plan for Maisie (continued)

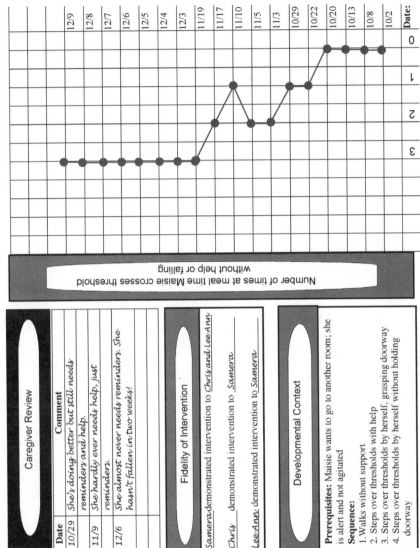

Number of times at meal time Maisie crosses threshold without help or falling

(Dates: 12/9, 12/8, 12/7, 12/6, 12/5, 12/4, 12/3, 11/19, 11/17, 11/10, 11/5, 11/3, 10/29, 10/22, 10/20, 10/13, 10/8, 10/2, Date: — scale 0, 1, 2, 3)

Caregiver Review

Date	Comment
10/29	She's doing better but still needs reminders and help.
11/9	She hardly ever needs help, just reminders.
12/6	She almost never needs reminders. She hasn't fallen in two weeks!

Fidelity of Intervention

Samera demonstrated intervention to Chris and Lee Ann

Chris _____ demonstrated intervention to Samera

Lee Ann demonstrated intervention to Samera

Developmental Context

Prerequisites: Maisie wants to go to another room; she is alert and not agitated

Sequence:
1. Walks without support
2. Steps over thresholds with help
3. Steps over thresholds by herself, grasping doorway
4. Steps over thresholds by herself without holding doorway

Note
You can reach Lee Ann Jung by e-mail at ljung@uky.edu

References
Bailey, D. B. (2003). Assessing family resources, priorities, and concerns. In M. McLean, M. Wolery, & D. Bailey (Eds.) *Assessing infants and preschoolers with special needs*. (3rd ed.). (pp. 172-203). New York: Merrill.

Bailey, D. B., & Wolery, M. (1992). *Teaching infants and preschoolers with disabilities* (2nd ed.). New York: Merrill.

Bernheimer, L. P., & Keogh, B. K. (1995). Weaving interventions into the fabric of everyday life: An approach to family assessment. *Topics in Early Childhood Special Education, 15*, 415-433.

Blasco, P. M. (2001). Curriculum and teaching strategies in early intervention. In P. M. Blasco (Ed.), *Early intervention services for infants, toddlers, and their families* (pp. 191-212). Boston: Allyn & Bacon.

Bricker, D., & Cripe, J. (1992). *An activity-based approach to early intervention*. Baltimore: Paul H. Brookes.

Bricker, D., Pretti-Frontczak, K., & McComas, N. (1998). *An activity-based approach to early intervention* (2nd ed.). Baltimore: Paul H. Brookes.

Cripe, J. W., & Venn, M. L. (1997). Family-guided routines for early intervention services. *Young Exceptional Children, 1*(1), 18-26.

Dunst, C. J., Bruder, M. B., Trivette, C. M., Raab, M., & McLean, M. (2001). Natural learning opportunities for infants, toddlers, and preschoolers. *Young Exceptional Children, 4*(3), 18-25.

Dunst, C. J., Herter, S., Shields, H., & Bennis, L. (2001). Mapping community-based natural learning opportunities. *Young Exceptional Children, 4*(4), 16-25.

Gargiulo, R. M., & Kilgo, J. (2000). *Young children with special needs*. New York: Delmar.

Harbin, G., McWilliam, R., Shaw, D., Buka, S., Sideris, J., Kockaek, T., Gallagher, J., Tocci, L., West, T., & Clark, K. (1998). *Implementing federal policy for young children with disabilities: How are we doing?* Chapel Hill, NC: University of North Carolina, Frank Porter Graham Child Development Center, Early Childhood Research Institute on Service Utilization.

Jung, L. A., & Baird, S. M. (2003). Effects of service coordinator variables on individualized family service plans. *Journal of Early Intervention 25*, 45-57.

McBride, S. L., & Peterson, C. (1997). Home-based early intervention with families of children with disabilities: Who is doing what? *Topics in Early Childhood Special Education, 17*, 209-233.

McGee, G. G., Morrier, M. J., & Daly, T. (1999). An incidental teaching approach to early intervention for toddlers with autism. *The Association for Persons With Severe Disabilities, 24*, 133-146.

McWilliam, R. A. (1992). *Family-centered intervention planning: A routines-based approach*. Tuscon, AZ: Communication Skill Builders.

McWilliam, R. A. (2000). It's only natural … to have early intervention in the environments where it's needed. In S. Sandall & M. Ostrosky (Eds.), *YEC monograph series no. 2: Natural environments and inclusion* (pp. 17-26). Longmont, CO: Sopris West.

Mullis, L. (2002). Natural environments: A letter from a mother to friends, families, and professionals. *Young Exceptional Children, 5*(3), 21-26.

Noonan, M. J., & McCormick, L. (1993). *Early intervention in natural environments: Methods and procedures*. Pacific Grove, CA: Brooks/Cole.

Prizant, B., & Bailey, D. (1992). Facilitating the acquisition and use of communication skills. In D. B. Bailey & M. Wolery (Eds.), *Teaching infants and preschoolers with disabilities* (2nd ed.) (pp. 299-362). New York: Merrill.

Rule, S., Losardo, A., Dinnebeil, L., Kaiser, A., & Rowland, C. (1998). Translating research on naturalistic instruction into practice. *Journal of Early Intervention, 21*, 283-293.

Schwartz, I. S., & Rodriguez, P. B. (2001). A few issues to consider: The who, what, and where of family support. *Journal of Early Intervention, 2*, 19-21.

Tisot, C. M., & Thurman, S. K. (2002). Using behavior setting theory to define natural settings: A family-centered approach. *Infants and Young Children, 14*(3), 65-71.

Washington, K., Schwartz, I. S., & Swinth, Y. (1994). Physical and occupational therapists in naturalistic early childhood settings: Challenges and strategies for training. *Topics in Early Childhood Special Education, 14*, 333-349.

Wolery, M. (2000). Recommended practices in child-focused interventions. In S. Sandall, M. E. McLean, & B. J. Smith (Eds.), *DEC recommended practices in early intervention/early childhood special education.* (pp. 29-38). Longmont, CO: Sopris West.

Wolery, M., Brashers, M. S., & Neitzel, J. C. (2002). Ecological congruence assessment for classroom activities and routines: Identifying goals and intervention practices in child care. *Topics in Early Childhood Special Education, 14*, 131-142.

Entering Preschool:

Supporting Family Involvement in the Age Three Transition

D. Sarah Hadden, Ph.D.
University of Wisconsin-Eau Claire

Meet Sinead, a three-year old girl who just started preschool. For the first year of her life Sinead stayed home with her father, who took care of her while her mother worked. When Sinead's father went back to work shortly after her first birthday, Sinead started attending a neighborhood in-home child care with two other children her age. When Sinead turned three, her family decided that they wanted her to have more experiences in group settings, so they enrolled her in a preschool program three mornings per week. They selected a preschool that was only a few miles from her child care provider's home. Friends had sent their daughter to the same preschool and Sinead's family thought that it would be a good environment for her. Sinead's mother took her to preschool in the morning and then her child care provider picked her up just before lunch. At first, both Sinead and her family were a bit anxious about her attending preschool. Knowing this, her mother arranged to stay with her the first morning. The second day of preschool, her mother stayed for the first half-hour. The third day, Sinead told her mother that she didn't need to stay at all. She announced that she was a big girl and could go to preschool by herself! Sinead's transition to preschool was smooth and uneventful. When asked whether or not she had any concerns about Sinead going to preschool, her mother laughed and said, "No. She's pretty independent and gets along well with others. She'll do fine."

Now, let's meet Luke. Luke is also three-years old, and like Sinead, he has just started preschool. However, Luke has a rare genetic condition that resulted in his having multiple disabilities. He is nonambulatory and communicates through facial expressions and gestures. In addition, he has several medical concerns. Luke wears back and leg braces and must be tube fed.

While Sinead's family had few concerns about her transition to pre-school, Luke's family had many concerns. Luke had received early intervention services through a birth-to-three agency since his diagnosis at five months of age. A team of specialists, including a speech therapist, an occupational therapist, a physical therapist, and an early intervention teacher came to his home each week to work with him and give his parents ideas on how to support their son's development. His parents were happy with the early intervention services and questioned why they must move to a new program. Preschool seemed like such a big step and they worried about what they could do to ease Luke's transition into the new setting.

Transitions are a normal part of life and it is not uncommon for children in our culture to transition to preschool at age three or four and then to kindergarten at age five. However, young children with special needs may make additional transitions (Hanson et al., 2000). Some will make the transition from a neonatal intensive care unit (NICU) to home, from home to birth-to-three early intervention services, and then from birth-to-three to preschool.

Difficulties Associated With Transitions

While change of any kind can be problematic for young children with special needs, research suggests that the transition from a birth-to-three program to preschool can be particularly stressful (Hanson et al., 2000; Rosenkoetter, Hains, & Fowler, 1994). There are many reasons why this transition can be difficult. Birth-to-three early intervention programs, which serve infants and toddlers, are governed by Part C of the Individuals with Disabilities Education Act (IDEA), while preschool special education services are governed by Part B of IDEA (Individuals with Disabilities Education Amendments, 1997). By law young children with disabilities must exit Part C programs upon their third birthday, and if eligible for continued special education services, enter a Part B program. This move must take place even though some families may not necessarily want to change service providers (Hanson et al., 2000; Sweeden, 2001). It is not unusual for families to express concerns about the change in services that occurs when their children turn three (Hanline, 1988; Rosenkoetter et al., 1994). These concerns may

While change of any kind can be problematic ... research suggests that the transition from a birth-to-three program to preschool can be particularly stressful ....

be heightened when children move to an inclusive preschool, as these settings may place additional demands on young children with special needs (Ostrosky, Donegan, & Fowler, 1997).

Many changes occur when a child moves from a birth-to-three early intervention program to a preschool program (Hadden & Fowler, 2001; Hains, Rosenkoetter, & Fowler, 1991; Rosenkoetter et al., 1994). One of the most obvious differences has to do with the location and model of service delivery. Birth-to-three early intervention programs typically provide services in the home or child care setting. An individualized family service plan (IFSP), which identifies a family's priorities, resources, and concerns related to their child's development, guides services and the family is an integral part of the program. In contrast, preschool special education services, or Part B programs, are generally delivered within a school setting, whether it is a public school, a Head Start program, or a community preschool. In most states, the IFSP is discontinued and the individualized education program (IEP), which focuses on educationally relevant goals and objectives, is developed. While parents are a part of the IEP team, their role in service delivery is less central. Families may also experience other changes including differences in eligibility criteria, a decreased emphasis on family involvement, and in many cases, the loss of service coordination as a designated responsibility of one professional (Rosenkoetter et al., 1994).

Luke's parents worried about the changes they would experience when Luke exited the birth-to-three early intervention program. He seemed too young to go to school, and since he couldn't talk, they were unsure how they would know how he was doing. Would the new staff be able to interpret his gestures and facial expressions to know what he wanted? Luke's therapies were critical to his overall development. How would his parents know how to carry over the goals into the home if they weren't there to observe the therapists working with Luke? Finally, they wondered how they could ensure that his new program was meeting his developmental needs. Fortunately for Luke's family, the birth-to-three providers collaborated with the staff from the preschool program to help Luke's family prepare for the change in services.

The remainder of this article discusses ways in which professionals and families can work together to facilitate transitions for young children with special needs.

Effective Transition Planning

Federal regulations require transition planning when a child turns three and exits a birth-to-three early intervention program. According to IDEA, the following steps must be taken when a young child turns three: (1) the child's IFSP must be amended to include a transition plan; (2) parents must receive information about the transition process and future placement options; (3) children must be prepared for the change in service delivery; and (4) with parental permission, the early intervention agency must share with the local education agency pertinent information about the child (Individuals with Disabilities Education Amendments, 1997).

IDEA encourages active family involvement throughout the transition period, and indeed, family involvement is a critical component of successful transition planning (Bruder & Chandler, 1996; Rosenkoetter et al., 1994; Rous, Hemmeter, & Schuster, 1994). There are many roles that families may take throughout the transition period, and families should be given the opportunity to be involved in their child's transition to whatever extent they desire. First and foremost, providers should help families learn about the transition process. Providing information about the transition is crucial, as research indicates that families who are knowledgeable about the transition process experience less stress than families who lack information (Hamblin-Wilson & Thurman, 1990). Furthermore, families who are educated about the transition process are more likely to take an active role in decision making (Hanson et al., 2000). Providers can assist families to engage in a variety of other activities including, but not limited to, ensuring that the IFSP includes a transition plan, visiting potential programs, and helping to make decisions regarding their child's educational goals and future placement. Table 1 provides information on ways in which families may elect to be involved in planning their child's transition. It also presents strategies that professionals can use to promote active family involvement.

... [F]amilies should be given the opportunity to be involved in their child's transition to whatever extent they desire. First and foremost, providers should help families learn about the transition process.

It is useful to think about transition planning as a two-step process. First, there is the planning phase, which encompasses the wide variety of activities that take place prior to the child's third birthday. The second

Table 1: Ways That Families May be Involved in Their Child's Transition

Ways that families may be involved in their child's transition	Strategies professionals can use to promote family involvement
• Learn about the transition process	• Provide information about the transition process, including a timeline of activities
• Participate on the team that plans the transition	• Give families information on ways they can participate
• Help develop the transition plan for the IFSP	• Identify activities that will help the family prepare for the change in services
• Participate in evaluating the child for continuing eligibility for the next program	• Discuss information needed for assessment • Invite parents to participate in the assessment
• Identify goals that help prepare the child and the family for the change in services	• Provide information on the differences between early intervention and preschool services
• Visit potential programs	• Arrange visits to potential programs
• Help make decisions about IEP goals and objectives	• Explain the difference between IFSP and IEP • Learn about family priorities, concerns, and goals for their child
• Assist in making decisions regarding placement	• Ask the family to share their ideas and preferences about placement
• Share information about the child with the preschool staff	• Invite the family to visit before the start date • Ask about the child's preferences and abilities

Adapted with permission from Hadden & Fowler, 2001.

phase is the follow-up phase in which supports are provided to the child and family as they move into the new setting and/or program.

Planning Phase

Federal regulations require that birth-to-three early intervention providers initiate the planning phase a minimum of three months (90 days) before the child's third birthday. However, some researchers have suggested that planning should begin six to 12 months prior to the third birthday (Hanline, 1988; McDonald, Kysela, Siebert, McDonald, & Chambers, 1989). This extended timeframe ensures that families and professionals have adequate time to identify needs, as well as explore future placement options. This initial planning phase is the most intensive part of the transition process. Transition plans are developed, programs are visited, and the child and family are prepared for the change in services during this phase. The first column of Table 2 provides example activities for addressing the planning phase of the transition process. And, let's return to the vignette of Luke's transition as an example for understanding strategies and activities in which to engage during the planning phase.

Table 2: Sample Activities to be Done Throughout the Transition Process

Activities that take place prior to the child's third birthday	Activities that take place once the child begins preschool
• Learn about the transition process	• Share information with the new staff
• Amend the IFSP to include a transition plan	• Help the child adjust to the new schedule and routines
• Learn about the differences between 0-3 and preschool programs	• Arrange for favorite activities to take place at school (e.g., snacks, songs, games, etc.)
• Visit potential programs	• Be positive about the new program
• Talk to parents who have children in preschool	• With parental permission, arrange for communication between the early intervention providers and preschool staff
• Once selected, visit the new program and meet the new teacher	
• Have the child spend time at the new program	• Communicate with the new staff on a frequent and ongoing basis
• Prepare the child and family for the change in services	

Luke's family was actively involved throughout the entire transition process. While his parents had informal conversations with their birth-to-three early intervention providers about the transition from the time Luke began receiving early intervention services, the formal planning began approximately six months (180 days) before his third birthday. His mother explained, "His needs are so complex ... everyone felt that we needed additional time to get everything set up. Any program he would go to needed time to get ready. We also hoped that by having a lot of lead time that his new teacher and therapists would have the chance to come and observe Luke and see what worked best for him."

The birth-to-three early intervention program and the school district worked together to help Luke's family prepare for his entry into preschool. For example, the birth-to-three early intervention program convened a meeting with the school district to develop his transition plan. At this meeting, the district gave Luke's family information about assessment, eligibility, and the kinds of programs they offered. Once the formal referral was made, the birth-to-three program arranged times for Luke's family to visit different district programs. A representative from the district contacted his family prior to his evaluation. They decided that Luke's parents would participate in his evaluation. "Luke's behaviors can be somewhat difficult to interpret," his mother said. "It was nice to be there during his evaluation to explain his communication and behaviors to others. Also, the school district accepted some of the assessments that had been done in early intervention. That was nice too, because we did not have to go through some of the same testing all over again!"

Once eligibility for continued services was established, Luke's family participated in the discussion about placement. Determining the appropriate placement for a preschooler with a disability can be challenging. IDEA contains a provision stating that children with disabilities should receive services in the least restrictive environment (LRE). This means that children with special needs should have the opportunity to be educated with peers who do not have disabilities. Unfortunately, few school districts provide educational services to typically developing three- and four-year olds (Hanline, 1993). Thus, a family's options for preschool services may be limited to established programs within their own community (Hanson et al., 2000).

Luke's district was among the many districts that do not provide universal preschool. Therefore, the only option that was extended to Luke's family was to enroll him in a district-run preschool class for children with special needs. It was determined at his IEP meeting that Luke would attend school four mornings per week. Luke's parents also decided to send Luke to a community-based early childhood program in the afternoon. This arrangement allowed their son to receive the intensive services he needed, while also giving him the opportunity to interact with typical peers. "We could have pushed for the district to provide services in the early childhood program," his mother mused, "but in truth, we thought the special education pre-school program was the best option for Luke. We had visited the classroom and were impressed with the services there ... especially all of the assistive technology. We felt that the special education program was the right place for him at that time."

Once Luke's placement was decided, Pam, Luke's new teacher, invited his parents to visit the classroom. She also asked the therapists who would work with Luke to be present. This visit allowed Luke's parents to share information about him with his future team. At that meeting, they decided that all of the team members would observe Luke prior to his first day of school. Pam was interested in learning how to tube feed Luke and interpret his gestures and facial expressions. The thera-pists wanted to observe therapy sessions in the birth-to-three early intervention program. They also agreed to implement a home-school communication notebook to keep his family updated on his progress.

When the time came for Luke to go to school, his family felt comfort-able. According to his mother, "We had planned really well. The help we received from the birth-to-three early intervention program and the school district let us know exactly what we were getting into and that made us feel good! Of course we felt a little bit of trepidation, but not much more than we felt when his older sisters started preschool."

Follow-Up Phase

Transition support planning should not end once the child turns three and preschool services begin. Children with special needs may take more time to adjust to a new setting than do their typical peers (Hadden & Fowler, 2001; Hanline, 1993). Continued efforts may be necessary to ease the child's and the family's adjustment. For a transition to be truly successful, it is important that the family and providers plan for those events that occur at the time the child exits the birth-to-three program, as well as plan for the timeframe immediately after preschool begins. The second column of Table 2 provides activities for addressing the second phase of the transition process, the follow-up phase. Let's see how this follow-up phase was addressed with Luke's family.

Luke's first day of preschool arrived. As planned, Luke's mother took him to school. The district had offered transportation, but it was easier for his mother to take him than to juggle his bus schedule with that of his siblings. "Plus," his mother said, "that way I got to see his teacher every morning!" Luke's mother found that the frequent communication she had with the staff, both in person and through the communication notebook, was crucial for the success of Luke's transition. Further, she continued to have informal contact with the early intervention providers for several weeks as she shared with them how Luke was adjusting. The preschool teachers had ready access to these same providers as questions arose that his mother did not feel she could fully respond to alone.

Conclusion

Luke's parents took an extremely active role in his transition. In fact, his mother indicated that she and her husband really "led the process." Some families, like Luke's, may take the lead in the transition planning process, while others may not be comfortable doing so. It is important that professionals recognize that families may choose to participate in various ways and provide them choices about the role they would like to play. Factors that may influence how a family participates include the characteristics of the family, the child's special needs, family priorities and concerns, and the family's culture and beliefs (Lynch & Hanson, 1998). Because respect for families' preferences is an underlying assumption for early childhood services (Sandall, McLean, & Smith, 2000), it is critical that providers honor the different roles that families may elect to take in their child's transition.

For a transition to be truly successful, it is important that the family and providers plan for those events that occur at the time the child exits the birth-to-three program, as well as plan for the timeframe immediately after preschool begins.

The beginning of preschool means different things for different families. Some families, like Sinead's, may see preschool as a sign that their child is growing up and becoming more independent. They may welcome the new opportunities that preschool affords their children. Other families, particularly those of children with special needs, may view the move with less certainty. Instead of being excited that their child will have the chance to meet a new circle of friends, they may be worried about whether or not their child will be accepted by his or her new peers (Hains et al., 1991; Hanline, 1993). While the family of a typically developing child may be pleased that their child will participate in creative activities such as music and art, parents of a child with a disability may wonder if their child's needs will be adequately addressed within the framework of those activities (Hanline, 1993).

The federal mandate for transition planning should help ensure that children and families have a smooth transition between birth-to-three early intervention and preschool programming. However, research indicates that many parents experience their child's transition from birth-to-three to preschool as an event that happened to them rather than as a process in which they were key players and decision makers (Hanson et al., 2000). Other researchers have suggested that too often, transitions in early childhood are viewed as an event driven by paperwork rather than as a process designed to help prepare children and families for a change in services (Prendeville & Ross-Allen, 2002). Providers who assist families to plan actively for the activities that take place throughout the transition period help to ensure that the transition is indeed a process in which professionals respect the wishes and desires of the families, thereby minimizing the stress and uncertainty that many families may feel.

Notes

The author wishes to thank Deb Kavanagh of Eau Claire, WI, for graciously sharing her family's story. You can reach D. Sarah Hadden by e-mail at haddends@uwec.edu

References

Bruder, M. B., & Chandler, L. K. (1996). Transition. In S. L. Odom & M. E. McLean (Eds.), *Early intervention/early childhood special education: Recommended practices* (pp. 287-307). Austin, TX: PRO-ED.

Hadden, D. S., & Fowler, S. A. (2001). Planning transitions to support inclusion. In K. Allen & I. Schwartz (Eds.), *The exceptional child: Inclusion in early childhood education* (pp. 316-332). Albany, NY: Delmar.

Hains, A. H., Rosenkoetter, S. E., & Fowler, S. A. (1991). Transition planning with families in early intervention programs. *Infants and Young Children, 3*(4), 38-47.

Hamblin-Wilson, C., & Thurman, S. K. (1990). The transition from early intervention to kindergarten: Parental satisfaction and involvement. *Journal of Early Intervention, 14*, 55-61.

Hanline, M. F. (1988). Making the transition to preschool: Identification of parent needs. *Journal of the Division for Early Childhood, 12*, 98-107.

Hanline, M. F. (1993). Facilitating integrated preschool service delivery transitions for children, families, and professionals. In C. A. Peck, S. L. Odom, & D. B. Bricker (Eds.), *Integrating young children with disabilities into community programs: Ecological perspectives on research and implementation* (pp. 133-146). Baltimore: Paul H. Brookes.

Hanson, M. J., Beckman, P. J., Horn, E., Marquart, J., Sandall, S. R., Greig, D., & Brennan, E. (2000). Entering preschool: Family and professional experiences in this transition process. *Journal of Early Intervention, 23*, 279-293.

Individuals with Disabilities Education Amendments of 1997, PL 105-17. *U.S. Statutes at Large, 108.*

Lynch, E. W., & Hanson, M. J. (1998). *Developing cultural competence.* Baltimore: Paul H. Brookes.

McDonald, L., Kysela, G. M., Siebert, P., McDonald, S., & Chambers, J. (1989). Parent perspectives: Transition to preschool. *Teaching Exceptional Children, 18*, 123-129.

Ostrosky, M. M., Donegan, M. M., & Fowler, S. A. (1997). Facilitating transitions across home, community, and school: Developing effective service delivery models. In A. M. Wetherby, S. F. Warren, & J. Reichle (Eds.), *Transitions in prelinguistic communication: Preintentional to intentional and presymbolic to symbolic* (pp. 437-460). Baltimore: Paul H. Brookes.

Prendeville, J., & Ross-Allen, J. (2002). The transition process in the early years: Enhancing speech-language pathologists' perspectives. *Language, Speech, and Hearing Services in Schools, 33,* 130-139.

Rosenkoetter, S. E., Hains, A. H., & Fowler, S. A. (1994). *Bridging early services for children with special needs and their families: A practical guide for transition planning.* Baltimore: Paul H. Brookes.

Rous, B., Hemmeter, M. L., & Schuster, J. (1994). Sequenced transitions to education in the public schools: A systems approach to transition planning. *Topics in Early Childhood Special Education, 14,* 374-393.

Sandall, S., McLean, M. E., & Smith, B. J. (2000). *DEC recommended practices in early intervention/early childhood special education.* Longmont, CO: Sopris West.

Sweeden, B. (2001). Birth-to-three transition: One family's story. *Young Exceptional Children, 4*(2), 12-14.

The Notebook System

Developing Language and Literacy While
Strengthening Home-School Communication

Rebecca B. McCathren, Ph.D.
University of Missouri

Maria Long, M.Ed.
Columbia Public Schools, Columbia, MO

Communicating frequently and effectively with family members is one of the most important responsibilities of preschool teachers (Eldridge, 2001). This is true for anyone who works with young children, but is even more important for teachers of children with disabilities, children who may not have the necessary language to talk about their day. Some ways teachers communicate with families are sending notes home weekly or bi-weekly, talking with parents as they drop off or pick up their children, or calling parents to communicate information about school and to receive information about home. Home visits may also be scheduled routinely. The effectiveness of these strategies depends on individual needs and circumstances of both the family and the teacher.

There are many reasons for having less communication between home and school than both teachers and families desire (Powell, 1989). First, many family members are in the work force and not available to visit the classroom during the school day. Second, many preschoolers in early childhood special education (ECSE) ride to and from school on a bus so teachers and family members do not see each other routinely at drop-off and pick-up times. Third, some family members have difficulty reading and writing in English, which makes written communication more difficult. Finally, time is at a premium for both families and teachers, and finding the time to communicate in meaningful ways competes with other demands and responsibilities. Many teachers are looking for new ways to keep the lines of communication open without taking a lot of time from their busy days. One way of doing this is to use a strategy we call the Notebook System (Long, 2002).

We have five goals for this article. First, we describe the Notebook System and how it can be implemented in a preschool classroom. Second, we discuss the purpose of our Notebook System and how it came to be developed. Third, we provide a brief review of the empirical literature that supports the use of a Notebook System. Fourth, we discuss the learning opportunities provided to children through the use of this system and, finally, we provide feedback from parents whose children have used the Notebook System.

Description of the Notebook System

The notebook is a child-sized loose-leaf notebook made from laminated card stock, one per child. The notebook has picture sentences on each page with a box with Velcro® where the child puts a symbol (e.g., photograph) that completes the sentence. For example, after snack each child picks the symbol for what he or she ate and fills in the sentence, "Today I ate ____." In this snack example, the word "ate" is accompanied by a photograph of a child holding a spoon up to his open mouth. During "review" (the final moments of each activity) the child completes the pages: "Today I played with ___" (with pictures of objects representing toys and activities) and "Today my buddies were ___" (with space for pictures of four people, including both classmates and classroom adults). The other sentence pages include: "Today I drank ___," "Today I made ___," "Today my job was ___," and "Today was a ____ day." An additional page can be designated for families to communicate with the teacher: "Last night I ____." Symbols can be sent home that represent some of the activities that might take place in the evening, such as, "took a bath," "played with my sister/brother," or "went to McDonalds." Symbols depicting evening events can be individualized for each family with input from the family. On each page there is also a photograph depicting the verb or other important words in each sentence. For example, "played with," "my job," and "my buddies" all have pictures that represent the words (see Figure 1). At the back of the notebook there is a page labeled "Teacher Comments" and another labeled "Parent Comments." Each has a small stack of 3 x 3" sticky-backed notepads for written communication. These notes are then transferred into parent/teacher contact logs at the beginning or ending of each day for future reference.

Figure 1: Sample Pages From the Notebook System

The notebooks are taken home at the end of each day and shared with families. The notebook helps children remember what they did and provides families with information that allows them to ask questions and talk with their children about the day. Because the format of the notebook is the same each day, verbal children are soon able to "read" their notebook to their parents and siblings. For children from families who do not speak English fluently, adding words in the home language along with the English words will help make a stronger connection among activities, classroom language, and the home language. Families from cultures who are not familiar with the structure or format of American preschools may better understand their child's experiences while in school. This will help families support their child to make connections between experiences at home and at school.

Each evening parents may help children fill in the pages that describe the family's activities. This step provides teachers with information that allows them to ask questions and talk with children about home routines and activities. Teachers can highlight the previous evening's events and help the children make connections between home and school. It also can help teachers get a better sense of home and school similarities and differences for each family.

When developing a new system, the teacher must decide on the types of symbols to use. Possible choices for preschoolers include printed words, photographs, line drawings, or commercially produced symbols. This decision must take into account the developmental level of the individual children in the classroom. Pictures of actual objects are generally easier for most children to interpret and are often the first choice for preschoolers. For children who are nonverbal, the pictures provide a communication system that allows them to begin to use symbols to make their wants and needs known. For children who are verbal, the pictures support their language and the text that accompanies each picture helps children begin to make the connection between text and pictures in a meaningful way. Two of the more widely utilized computer programs for generating symbols are Mayer-Johnson's *Boardmaker* and *Writing With Symbols 2000* (Mayer-Johnson, Inc., 2003a, 2003b). Both programs are user-friendly and contain line drawings for almost any object or activity imaginable. Both systems also allow users to import digital pictures.

Purpose and Development of the Notebook System

The Notebook System was developed as a way to communicate with families without taking a lot of time in the day away from interacting with the children. Through the Notebook System, children take an active role in relating information to their families about their day. The Notebook System was piloted during a summer school session with a small number of children in an ECSE classroom. The eight children ranged in age from three to five years, all with disabilities and eligible for the extended school year program. Initially the notebook had eight

Through the Notebook System, children take an active role in relating information to their families about their day.

pages (four pages front and back). These pages included information about the date; toys with which the students played; items they ate, drank, made; and what kind of day they had (e.g., great, okay, rough). There were also pages for parent and teacher comments. During the summer school session, surveys were distributed to discover what additional information families might want about their children's days. Seven of the eight families responded. All of the families who responded were very positive about using the notebook as a means of communication. As a result of their input, additions were made to the notebook. These additional pages addressed the child's playmates (or "buddies") and classroom jobs. The Notebook System was then added as a regular component of the curriculum to the morning and afternoon sessions of an integrated ECSE classroom.

Empirical Support for the Notebook System

The Notebook System is a child-facilitated system that utilizes pictures and printed words to support communication between families and classroom staff. In addition, the System provides support for the language and literacy skills of preschoolers. The notebook is used throughout the day as children make choices about what they plan to do and then review what they actually did.

Although the specific practice described in this article has not been empirically validated, the Notebook System is based on empirically validated practices. These practices include: the High/Scope "Plan-Do-Review" process (High/Scope Educational Research Foundation, 1999); Alternative Augmentative Communication (AAC) systems (Mirenda, 2001; Mirenda & Erickson, 2000); visual schedules and classroom supports (National Research Council, 2001; Scott, Clark, & Brady, 2000); and the importance of positive shared experiences with meaningful text for the development of literacy (see Owocki, 2001 for a discussion). A brief discussion of the research follows.

High/Scope is an empirically validated educational approach that was developed in the 1960s as a cognitively oriented, Piagetian-based curriculum that was initially implemented with children living in poverty (Hohmann, Banet, & Weikart, 1979). The most powerful validation of the curriculum has been demonstrated by the outcome studies that have followed the participants from preschool through age 27 (Schweinhart, Barnes, Weikart, Barnett, & Epstein, 1993; Schweinhart & Weikart, 1993). One of the processes central to the High/Scope curriculum is the "Plan-Do-Review" sequence (High/Scope Educational Research Foundation, 1999). In the "plan" step, each adult in the classroom works with a small group of children and before choice time helps them plan what they are going to do first in the independent play period. Children indicate what they are going to do through a variety of means. For example, children may point to a toy or area of the classroom, tell the adult the activity or child with whom they want to play, or draw what they want to do (High/Scope Educational Research Foundation, 1996). Adults ask questions and converse with children in order to extend their thinking and to clarify their ideas. The next step, "do," involves the children carrying out their plans. During "review," children reflect on what they did and communicate their activities to the adult. This is done verbally (telling what they did) or through other means, such as drawing a picture or showing a product (High/Scope Educational Research Foundation, 1996).

Using the Notebook System children choose pictures of their buddies or the activity with which they would like to play. This represents the "plan" process. For children who are verbal, the adult asks questions to help expand their ideas. With children who are English Language Learners (ELL) or those with language delays, the adult labels the picture(s) the child has selected and may prompt for imitation of the language model. Once children select a picture, place it in their notebook, and interact with an adult about their "plan," they are free to "do" the activity. After the independent play period, children meet back with one of the classroom adults and "review" what they have done. If they followed their initial plan, they "read" their notebook with the adult and transition to the next activity. If children did not follow their initial plan, or the majority of the independent play period was spent engaged in an activity or with playmates not initially selected, children now choose the pictures that more closely represent what they did and then "read" their notebook with the adult. Again, classroom adults discuss each child's activities at the level most appropriate for that child. For some children this may entail conversations, drawings, or dramatic enactments. For other children, the adult may simply provide the appropriate labels or names for each of the pictures chosen.

Communication systems using graphic symbols have been successfully used to augment both receptive and expressive language for children with autism, mental retardation, and other developmental disabilities that interfere with the development of communication and language (see Mirenda, 2001 and Mirenda & Erickson, 2000 for reviews related to persons with autism). One of the more recently marketed and frequently used systems is the Picture Exchange Communication System (PECS) (Frost & Bondy, 1996). PECS is designed for children with autism or other disabilities that affect communication and social behavior. Initially children are taught to use pictures to request desired objects or activities. This allows children who are not yet able to speak an easily interpretable way to make their needs known. PECS is an AAC (Augmentative and Alternative Communication) system that is easy to implement and typically does not require extensive adult training. It is functional for the child, prerequisite skills are minimal, and it is easily adapted for individual likes and dislikes. Although PECS is initially used to obtain desired objects, it can be expanded and used to comment and to respond. In the training manual, Bondy and Frost (1994) reported that 59% of the 66 nonverbal preschool children who used PECS for more than a year developed independent, functional speech. Similar results were reported by Schwartz, Garfinkle, and Bauer (1998), who found that 44% of the 31 nonverbal preschoolers in their study acquired unprompted, nonecholalic speech while using PECS.

PECS and the Notebook System are complementary strategies. The pictures or symbols used in the notebook should be the same ones used in PECS for any particular child. Each child who is using PECS to communicate continues to do this throughout the day. At the end of each of the activities, the PECS symbol that represents the child's choice is placed in the appropriate spot in the notebook. For example, at snack time the PECS symbols are used for the child to request food items or a particular kind of drink. Small portions are given making it likely that the child will request more than once, which provides more communication practice. At the end of snack time, the PECS symbols are placed in the appropriate spots in the notebook and the child and adult "read" those pages together.

Jaleel is a five-year old boy with general developmental delays and limited speech intelligibility (articulation). Jaleel has participated in the Notebook System for the past two months. He often selects individual picture symbols in order to clarify his wants and needs when he encounters difficulty communicating with others. On a recent occasion, Jaleel was trying to indicate that he wanted to play on the computer. He attempted several times to communicate his intent to an adult and eventually went to a choice board, selected a picture of the computer, and brought it to the adult.

The use of visual supports and visual schedules are recommended for many children who have learning difficulties and are considered crucial for children with autism (Scott, Clark, & Brady, 2000). Children with autism typically have relative strengths in visual processing when compared to auditory processing. Therefore, pictures may be used to help children with autism understand the structure of the day, and to make the connection between spoken words, objects or activities, and the pictures. Using pictures to make requests and indicate preferences is an important strategy to reduce challenging behavior for children who are not able to use words to express wants or needs (National Research Council, 2001; Scott, Clark, & Brady, 2000). Integrating the Notebook System throughout the day provides children with autism and those requiring visual supports multiple opportunities to use pictures to make choices. In addition, the notebook can function as a visual schedule when the order of the pages follows the sequence of the day.

Kelley is a five-year old boy with a diagnosis of autism. Kelley has participated in the Notebook System for the past two years, and he thrives on the structure and predictability of the program. Each day, as Kelley arrives in the classroom, he eagerly opens his backpack, grasps his notebook, and begins to sort his symbols from the previous day without any adult prompting. Throughout the school day Kelley is able to complete his notebook by selecting appropriate symbols and placing them in the correct places. Since the pages of his notebook directly relate to the classroom schedule, Kelley is able to predict what will happen throughout the school day, which helps alleviate possible anxiety. Kelley is very independent in using the Notebook System, and will often remind his teachers when it is time to complete a page by saying, "I need my book please."

Much has been written describing the importance of early, positive literacy experiences for later development of reading skills. The Notebook System encompasses strategies and experiences that have been found to support the development of literacy skills (Christie, Enz, Vukelich, & Mitchell, 2003; National Research Council, 1998; Owocki, 2001). These strategies include using predictable text, providing opportunities for the development of narrative skills by talking about daily events, having positive interactions with text, using pictures to support the meaning of text, and frequently engaging in literacy activities. The Notebook System provides many opportunities each day to engage in these activities at school and supports these kinds of interactions at home.

Connor is a typically developing five-year old boy who has participated as a peer model in a reverse-mainstream early childhood special education classroom for the past two years. Connor is able to "read" his notebook independently to family members and adults in the classroom. Connor has also developed some sight word recognition, and understands that groups of letters form words. Connor demonstrates left to right correspondence when reading, and is able to point to individual words as he "reads." Connor is able to independently follow the routine designated by the Notebook System, and he demonstrates responsibility in managing his personal notebook (e.g., placing it in his backpack, remembering to bring the notebook to school).

Learning Opportunities for Children

There are six steps to follow when using the Notebook System and each step provides opportunities for learning. Steps 1 and 2 are Symbol Selection and Symbol Placement. Children choose the symbols that represent their experiences. Children complete one page of their notebook after each "chunk" of the day (e.g., opening circle, free choice, and snack). As each activity is finished children choose the symbol that represents what they did during that segment of the day. For example, if Jeff played with Javier, Nadia, and Shamisa at free choice time, during "review" he would select their pictures from a symbol board that contained pictures

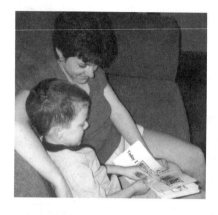

of all of the children in his class. The necessary support is provided for each child to accurately complete his or her page.

Step 3 is Shared Classroom Reading. Children can begin the day "reading" their page from home as the first activity of the day. Throughout the day each child "reads" the page he or she has completed to an adult in the classroom before transitioning to the next activity. Children who are verbal may be able to say all the words on the page using the pictures to help them. For children who are nonverbal or just beginning to use speech, the adult reads to the child, pointing to each word or picture and allowing plenty of time for the child to initiate a word or imitate what the adult has said.

Step 4 is Self-Evaluation. At the end of the day each child chooses one of three symbols that represents the kind of day he or she had at school. The children choose one of three thumbs: thumb up, which represents a great day; thumb sideways, which represents an okay day; or thumb down, which represents a rough day. The expectations are individualized and the behavioral goals are obtainable by each child. For children who are able to understand, the expectations are made explicit. Children who had a great day talk with the teacher about what they did that made it a great day. If a child did not have a great day, he or she talks with the teacher about what can happen tomorrow to have a great day.

Step 5 is Shared Home Reading. Once the children have completed their notebooks, they put them in their backpacks to take home to share them with their families. Parents may then have their child "read" to them, or they may read through the notebook with their child, asking questions and responding to what the child says. For children who are verbal, this kind of discussion supports the development of narrative skills as they tell about their playmates, what they made, and how they made it, for example. The pictures allow the parent to support and expand the narrative skills of the child as he or she tells about the day. Older and younger siblings also can participate in the reading of the notebook and can add to the conversation about their days, too. Family members and children can complete the home page(s) as part of the bedtime routine or in the morning before going to school.

Although the pictures that complete the sentences change each day, the structure of each sentence remains the same. This predictable text provides children with a positive learning experience as exemplified by their ability to "read" this book to members of their family. In addition, as children notice the regularities in the format and see groups of letters that consistently represent words, many will begin to develop a small sight word vocabulary. For children who are nonverbal, the notebook can be read to them by a family member. Children can be helped to point to the pictures that represent their day. Combining spoken words and pictures is one strategy for supporting the initial development of speech for children who are nonverbal. If something important has happened during the day and there are no pictures available to represent the learning, the teacher could write a note on the notepad in the back of the notebook, or the child might create his or her own picture of the important event. This item can be taped into the notebook.

Step 6 is Symbol Sorting. Each day as children arrive at school they remove their notebooks from their backpacks and sort the pictures into categories (e.g., things to eat). Each page of the notebook has a separate sorting tub, designated by the picture on the corresponding page. There is also a "buddy board" with rows of pictures of each of the children in the class. Children need to identify the category and then place their pictures with the pictures in the appropriate category.

Feedback From Families

The purpose of the Notebook System was to develop an efficient and effective way to communicate with families about their children.

The purpose of the Notebook System was to develop an efficient and effective way to communicate with families about their children. In order to obtain feedback from families, surveys were distributed for each of two years. Families were asked if they thought the Notebook System was beneficial and why. In general, the response was positive. All families surveyed said they liked the communication system and many wrote comments. Both families of children with disabilities and children who are typically developing found the system of communication useful. For example, one mother of a verbal child with autism said, "Maria's book has been instrumental in communicating with my daughter. The book provides a predictable format and sequence, but with new information each day. As she reads to me about her day, my daughter will often add extra details without any prompts! It's definitely improved the quality of our conversations .... I love it!"

Another mother with a son with a developmental delay said, "Each and every day my son chooses the appropriate pictures from the classroom display and uses fine motor skills to place them on the appropriate pages. He knows the names of all of his friends; the visual cues are so helpful to him in talking about his day with his siblings and me. All three of my little children have enjoyed his book and the interaction among the three youngsters has been enhanced with this book. Talk with his siblings [both age 5] has been challenging for him [age 4]. They can know how his day went, see the pictures, and have a 'conversation' about his day with him. He feels 'so big' when he can share about his day."

A last example is from a mother of two sons, ages five and three: "Our older son is a peer model and this system has really helped him to explain his days at preschool and to begin word recognition. Our youngest son has developmental delays, specifically speech, and also some attention difficulties. The notebook system has been so helpful for him! He is very much a visual learner and loves to read books, and this system has given him the ability to 'read' us his day by showing us the pictures of what he did. He has been able to use this system for word recognition and loves to look at this book. He will initiate reading time every day after school by getting his notebook out of his backpack to show me his day!"

Implementing the Program

Implementing this program into a classroom requires preparation. However, using the System with children and families does not require a lot of time and does provide many benefits. Teachers may want to begin by including a page for one time of the day (e.g., choice time) rather than try to report on all aspects of the day. This will allow teachers to modify and adapt this system to meet the needs of the specific children and families in their program.

Symbols, notebooks, and sorting tubs and boards all must be created prior to beginning the program. It is important to have enough symbol choices so that there are two or three available in the room for each activity, which cuts down on wait time as children select and remove pictures for their notebooks.

In classrooms for young children the symbols of choice are often pictures. Digital cameras make it easy to create usable symbols. Photographs can be downloaded onto a computer and imported into a text box. Using an additional text box words can be added below the picture. It is important to remember to keep the picture simple. If possible, create a solid background so that there are few visual distractions. Line drawings and commercially produced symbols are more abstract than photographs but have the advantage of being less specific, and thus, more easily generalized to other settings. Once a symbol system is selected, all classroom items (including the foods and drinks at snack) must be labeled with the symbol and words to help the children associate the items with their symbols. White card stock is recommended for printing the symbols. Finally, each symbol is laminated with Velcro® attached to the back. Although initially time consuming, the pictures can be used throughout the school year and even from year to year.

Notebooks can be made in a variety of ways. However, it is important that the notebooks be appropriate for young children. Sharp edges should be rounded and the pages should be sturdy so they are not easily torn. In addition, notebooks should be small enough to be manageable by small hands. It is also important to have extra books in the classroom so children can maintain the classroom routine in the event a notebook is forgotten at home. Extra book pages are also nice to have in order to replace torn or damaged pages.

Conclusion

In conclusion, the Notebook System can be an effective way for teachers and families to communicate while facilitating the development of language and literacy for all children in the classroom.

Note

You can reach Rebecca B. McCathren by e-mail at mccathrenr@missouri.edu

References

Bondy, A., & Frost, L. (1994). The picture exchange communication system. *Focus on Autistic Behavior, 9*(3), 1-19.

Christie, J., Enz, B., Vukelich, C., & Mitchell, D. (2003). *Teaching language and literacy: Preschool through elementary grades* (2nd ed.). Boston: Allyn & Bacon.

Eldridge, D. (2001). Parent involvement: It's worth the effort. *Young Children, 56*(4), 65-69.

Frost, L. A., & Bondy, A. S. (1996). PECS: *The picture exchange communication system.* Cherry Hill, NJ: Pyramid Educational Consultants.

High/Scope Educational Research Foundation. (1996). *High/Scope training manual: Preschool teacher introduction.* Ypsilanti, MI: High/Scope Press.

High/Scope Educational Research Foundation. (1999). *High/Scope training manual: Preschool teacher introduction.* Ypsilanti, MI: High/Scope Press.

Hohmann, M., Banet, B., & Weikart, D. P. (1979). *Young children in action.* Ypsilanti, MI: High/Scope Press.

Long, M. (2002). *The notebook system: Child-facilitated notebook communication system.* Unpublished manuscript.

Mirenda, P. (2001). Autism, augmentative communication, and assistive technology: What do we really know? *Focus on Autism and Other Developmental Disabilities, 16*(3), 141-151.

Mirenda, P., & Erickson, K. A. (2000). Augmentative communication and literacy. In A. M. Wetherby & B. M. Prizant (Eds.), *Autism spectrum disorders: A communicative approach* (pp. 333-369). Baltimore: Paul H. Brookes.

Mayer-Johnson, Inc. (2003a). *Boardmaker.* Retrieved June 24, 2003, from the Internet: http://www.mayer-johnson.com.

Mayer-Johnson, Inc. (2003b). *Writing with symbols 2000.* Retrieved June 24, 2003, from the Internet: http://www.mayer-johnson.com.

National Research Council. (1998). *Preventing reading difficulties in young children.* Washington, DC: National Academy Press.

National Research Council. (2001). *Educating children with autism.* Washington, DC: National Academy Press.

Owocki, G. (2001). *Make way for literacy! Teaching the way young children learn.* Washington, DC: National Association for the Education of Young Children (NAEYC).

Powell, D. R. (1989). *Families and early childhood programs.* Washington, DC: National Association for the Education of Young Children (NAEYC).

Schwartz, I. S., Garfinkle, A. N., & Bauer, J. (1998). The picture exchange communication system: Communicative outcomes for young children with disabilities. *Topics in Early Childhood Special Education, 18,* 144-159.

Schweinhart, L. J., Barnes, H. V., Weikart, D. P., Barnett, W. S., & Epstein, A. S. (1993). *Significant benefits: The High/Scope Perry Preschool study through age 27.* Ypsilanti, MI: High/Scope Press.

Schweinhart, L. J., & Weikart, D. P. (1993). Success by empowerment: The High/Scope Perry Preschool study through age 27. *Young Children, 49*(1), 54-58.

Scott, J., Clark, C., & Brady, M. (2000). *Students with autism: Characteristics and instructional programming.* San Diego, CA: Singular Publishing.

Resources

Within Reason

Family-Based Practices

Here you'll find additional resources to support effective collaboration with families of young children and to assist in developing supports and services within everyday routines, activities, and places. These resources range in price. Many are within an individual's budget while others may be more suitable for acquisition by an agency or program.

Camille Catlett, M.A., University of North Carolina at Chapel Hill

Books

DEC Recommended Practices in Early Intervention/Early Childhood Special Education
edited by S. Sandall, M. E. McLean, & B. J. Smith (2000)

This book is a good and current source for information about recommended practices and strategies for using them. Chapter 4: "Recommended Practices in Family-Based Practices" by Carol M. Trivette and Carl J. Dunst offers definitions of terms, delineation of quality features, and a checklist to assess the extent to which personal or program practices are family-based.

Sopris West
4093 Speciality Place
Longmont, CO 80504
(800) 547-6747
FAX (888) 819-7767
http://www.sopriswest.com

DEC Recommended Practices Program Assessment: Improving Practices for Young Children With Special Needs and Their Families

by M. L. Hemmeter, G. E. Joseph, B. J. Smith, & S. Sandall (2000)

Help in assessing and improving the quality of services you provide to young children with disabilities and to their families is what this publication can provide. Chapter 2 is devoted to family-based practices and can be used to determine the strengths, needs, and supports of your program. Whether you work at a Head Start, child care center, public school, or other early childhood/early intervention program, the examples and reproducible forms can help you enhance the quality of your program.

> Sopris West
> 4093 Speciality Place
> Longmont, CO 80504
> (800) 547-6747
> FAX (888) 819-7767
> http://www.sopriswest.com

Families, Professionals, and Exceptionality: Collaborating for Empowerment

by A. P. Turnbull & H. R. Turnbull, III (2001) (4th ed.)

The fourth edition of this classic and enduring text and its companion instructor's manual offer many activities related to family-centered practices. Each of 14 topical chapters (examples: historical and current roles of parents, family functions, referral and evaluation) includes ideas for student projects and class discussions, assignments, and discussion questions. A course syllabus, including requirements, topical outline, weekly assignments, and class project options, is also provided. An accompanying Web site (http://www.prenhall.com/turnbull) offers additional resources and ideas.

> Merrill/Prentice Hall
> Pearson Education
> One Lake Street
> Upper Saddle River, NJ
> (201) 236-7000
> Communications@pearsoned.com
> http://vig.prenhall.com

Fathers & Early Childhood Programs

by J. Fagan & G. Palm (2004)

Detailed information on practical strategies and useful approaches for involving fathers in early childhood programs are offered in this book. Readers will discover background information (e.g., history, theory, research) and resources (e.g., tools and instruments, models, case studies, examples of father involvement activities) for promoting meaningful paternal participation.

Delmar Learning
5 Maxwell Drive
P.O. Box 8007
Clifton Park, NY 12065-8007
(800) 347-7707
FAX (800) 487-8488
http://www.delmarlearning.com/index.asp

Partnerships in Family-Centered Care: A Guide to Collaborative Early Intervention

by P. Rosin, A. Whitehead, L. I. Tuchman, G. Jesien, A. Begun, & L. Irwin (1996)

Three interrelated sections focusing on family-centered care, team-building, and service coordination form the heart of this book. Each chapter features a story to facilitate creative problem solving on issues raised throughout the chapter. There is also a variety of instructional aides (e.g., objectives, activities, discussion questions) skillfully inter-woven with the content. This resource is much more than a textbook and has broad applicability for all early intervention disciplines.

Paul H. Brookes
P.O. Box 10624
Baltimore, MD 21285-0624
(800) 638-3775
FAX (410) 337-8539
http://www.pbrookes.com

A Path to Follow: Learning to Listen to Parents
by P. A. Edwards (1999)

When we learn to listen to the stories parents tell about their children and activities they engage in at home, we can learn about the strengths, needs, and resources of the family and child. The author explains that with this information, we can also learn about how to effectively involve parents in their children's education and to develop family/professional collaboration. Teachers, directors, and administrators, as well as faculty and students, can benefit greatly from this book because it not only discusses the importance of listening to families, but it outlines ways to get the kind of information you seek.

> Heinemann
> P.O. Box 6926
> Portsmouth, NH 03802-6926
> (800) 225-5800
> FAX (603) 431-2214
> custserv@heinemann.com
> http://www.heinemann.com

A Place to Begin: Working With Parents on Issues of Diversity
by J. Gonzalez-Mena & D. Pulido-Tobiassen (1999)

Have you ever wanted to bring up a potentially sensitive issue with a parent or have a conversation, but weren't sure how to begin? Have you ever wanted to learn more about a parent's ideas on childrearing? This resource may guide you in discovering effective methods and materials. Handouts are included in English, Spanish, Vietnamese, and Chinese.

> California Tomorrow
> 1904 Franklin Street, Suite 300
> Oakland, CA 94612
> (510) 496-0220, x 23
> FAX (510) 496-0225
> info@californiatomorrow.org
> http://www.californiatomorrow.org

Teaching Other People's Children: Literacy and Learning in a Bilingual Classroom
by C. Ballenger (1998)

What happens when a teacher does not share a cultural background with his or her young students? Ballenger's narrative shares the experiences of one North American teacher who spent three years teaching Haitian children in an inner-city preschool. This engaging account, which does a splendid job of enforcing the importance of thoughtful research, uses first person narrative to explore the complexities of family-based practices.

Teachers College Press
P.O. Box 20
Willliston, VT 05495-0020
(800) 575-6566
FAX (802) 864-7626
http://www.teacherscollegepress.com

Skilled Dialogue: Strategies for Responding to Cultural Diversity in Early Childhood
by I. Barrera, R. M. Corso, & D. Macpherson (2003)

Understanding how to respond to cultural diversity is one key to successful family-based practices. This resource gives early childhood professionals the knowledge they need to improve that understanding. Through this book, practitioners will better understand the challenges of collaboration with family members whose values, beliefs, and backgrounds differ from their own. Further, they will discover a repertoire of skills and strategies for reframing differences between practitioners and families. The chapter entitled "Respectful, Reciprocal, and Responsive Assessment" is a particularly rich and timely source of new ideas.

Paul H. Brookes
P.O. Box 10624
Baltimore, MD 21285-0624
(800) 638-3775
FAX (410) 337-8539
http://www.pbrookes.com

The Spirit Catches You and You Fall Down: A Hmong Child, Her American Doctors, and the Collision of Two Cultures
by A. Fadiman (1997)

The clash between a small county hospital in California and a refugee family from Laos over the care of Lia Lee, a Hmong child diagnosed with severe epilepsy, is chronicled in this book. Lia's parents and her doctors both want what is best for her, but the lack of understanding between them leads to tragedy. Good writing and a thoughtful reader's guide featuring questions for discussion make this a rich resource for learning about the complexities of family-based practices.

> Farrar, Straus, and Giroux
> 19 Union Square West
> New York, NY 10003
> (888) 330-8477
> sales@fsgbooks.com
> http://www.fsgbooks.com

Strengthening the Family-Professional Partnership in Services for Young Children
by R. N. Roberts, S. Rule, & M. Innocenti (1998)

This book explains the shift from professional-directed services to family-based practices. Various ways that families can participate are discussed in depth and include service coordination, preservice personnel preparation, program evaluation, and systems-level support. Brief case studies explain the realities (both the pain and joy) of parenting children with special needs and demonstrate how resourceful families can be for professionals and for themselves.

> Paul H. Brookes
> P.O. Box 10624
> Baltimore, MD 21285-0624
> (800) 638-3775
> FAX (410) 337-8539
> http://www.pbrookes.com

Supporting & Strengthening Families: Methods, Strategies, and Practices
by C. Dunst, C. Trivette, & A. Deal (1994)

The theory, methods, strategies, and practices involved in adopting an empowerment and family-centered resource approach to supporting families and strengthening individual and family functioning are championed in this book. Topics include the meaning and key characteristics of empowerment; family support programs; individual family support plans; family needs, strengths, and resources; and effective helpgiving practices.

Cambrid Brookline Books
P.O. Box 97
Newton Upper Falls, MA 02464
(800) 666-BOOK
FAX (617) 558-8011
http://www.brooklinebooks.com

Checklists and Measures

DEC Recommended Practices in Early Intervention/Early Childhood Special Education: Parent Checklist

What should parents (and professionals) look for as features of family-based programs and practices? Here's a concise list to use in identifying exemplary practices and targeting others for change and improvement.

http://www.dec-sped.org/pdf/recommendedpractices/parentchecklist.pdf

Family-Centered Services: Guiding Principles and Practices for Delivery of Family-Centered Services
by L. C. Pletcher & S. McBride (2000)

To assist practitioners and programs with the application of key principles of family-centered practice, these Iowa colleagues created an annotated checklist, which offers thoughtful, practical examples of how to support each principle. To obtain a copy, contact Linnie Hanrahan by phone (515-281-3021), FAX (515-242-6019) or e-mail (Linnie.Hanrahan@ed.state.ia.us).

Family Quality of Life Scale

The Beach Center on Disabilities at the University of Kansas has developed this instrument with which families rate the importance of, and their satisfaction with, 35 items organized into four domains of family life: Family Interaction, Parenting, Family Resources, and Supports for the Family Member With a Disability. Versions are currently available for research/program evaluation and for direct family-based application (e.g., developing IFSPs or other collaborative plans with families). For psychometric data or a draft copy of the measures, contact Denise Poston (denisep@ku.edu). Additional information is also available at the Beach Center Web site (http://www.beachcenter.org/). Click on "Research," and then enter "family quality of life" in the "Search" box.

Family-Professional Partnership Scale

Another recent Beach Center contribution is this instrument with which families rate the importance of, and their satisfaction with, 21 items organized into two domains of partnership: Professional-Child Relationships and Professional-Family Relationships. The scale has been used to help programs identify areas requiring improvement. For psychometric data or a draft copy of the measure, contact Denise Poston (denisep@ku.edu). Additional information is also available at the Beach Center Web site (http://www.beachcenter.org/). Click on "Research," and then enter "family-professional partnership" in the "Search" box.

Videotapes

Delivering Family-Centered, Home-Based Services
by L. Edelman (1991)

This videotape includes five vignettes, developed for viewing one at a time followed by discussions and activities (included in the facilitator's guide). Each vignette shows an interaction, then invites a discussion of how the interaction might have occurred in a more family-based manner. Each illustrates what happens when service providers fail to use family-based practices. Background on family-centered principles and ideas for additional activities are also included.

Kennedy Krieger Institute
Training and Products Division
7000 Tudsbury Road
Baltimore, MD 21244
(410) 298-9286
FAX (410) 298-9288
http://www.kennedykrieger.org/accessible/kki_misc.jsp?pid=1601

Family-Guided Activity-Based Intervention for Infants & Toddlers
by J. J. Cripe (1995)

This 20-minute videotape illustrates strategies through which parents and other caregivers can use natural learning opportunities to support family-based practices. The narration and examples are very clear and provide concise suggestions for paths to more effective family-based practices.

> Paul H. Brookes
> P.O. Box 10624
> Baltimore, MD 21285-0624
> (800) 638-3775
> FAX (410) 337-8539
> http://www.pbrookes.com

Just Being Kids: Supports and Services for Infants and Toddlers and Their Families in Everyday Routines, Activities, and Places
produced by L. Edelman (2001)

Supports and services for infants and toddlers with special needs are best provided in the context of families' everyday routines, activities, and places. Each of the six stories in this video demonstrates collaboration with a family to achieve meaningful goals for their child. Parents and providers reflect on their experiences in ways that offer examples for diverse audiences, including teachers, therapists, and service coordinators. A Facilitator's Guide offers background information on the stories, suggestions for discussion, and activities to enhance viewers' learning.

> Western Media Products
> P.O. Box 591
> Denver, CO 80201
> (800) 232-8902
> FAX (303) 455-5302
> http://www.media-products.com

One of the Family

by Early Connections for Infants, Toddlers, and Families, Colorado Department of Education (1998)

Four culturally diverse families, each with a young child with a disability, warmly describe the values that motivate them: including their children in all family activities, treating them as children first, expecting the most from them, looking for a normal family life, and choosing professionals who support their values. Use this video to get a fresh perspective on family-based practices.

> Western Media Products
> P.O. Box 591
> Denver, CO 80201
> (800) 232-8902
> FAX (303) 455-5302
> http://www.media-products.com

Web Resources

DEC Recommended Practices: Family-Based Practices Strand Reference List

Key research publications in peer-reviewed professional journals from 1990 through 1998 were identified through a national process facilitated by DEC. The references for articles related to family-based practices are offered at the URL listed below.

> http://www.dec-sped.org/images/word_documents/FamilyBasedStrand.doc

Family Village (A Global Community of Disability-Related Resources)

The Family Village community includes informational resources on specific diagnoses, communication connections, adaptive products and technology, adaptive recreational activities, education, worship, health issues, disability-related media and literature, and much more! The resources they feature are always changing, but the emphasis on supporting family-based practices remains constant.

> http://www.familyvillage.wisc.edu/

Family Voices

This Web site of families and friends speaking on behalf of children with special needs can be a great place to find resources and information. While much of the emphasis is on health issues, this site offers much more, including policy briefs, instructional resources, fact sheets, and information links.

http://www.familyvoices.org/

Family-Guided Approaches to Collaborative Early-Intervention Training and Services (FACETS)

The FACETS Web site was designed to support meaningful family participation and decision making in the intervention planning process. It offers strategies for ensuring effective interdisciplinary and interagency collaboration throughout the intervention process, along with "how-to" information and training for family members, early interventionists, related service providers, and administrators.

http://www.parsons.lsi.ukans.edu/facets/

FamilyNet

Covering relationships, parenting, and home life for gay, lesbian, bisexual, and transgender people and their families is the purpose of this Web site. It offers a range of information and resources that can be used to support family-based practices.

http://www.hrc.org/familynet/

Federation for Children With Special Needs

The Federation was organized in 1975 as a coalition of parent groups representing children with a variety of disabilities. Their Web site offers a variety of services and resources to parents, parent groups, and others who are concerned with supporting family-based practices.

http://www.fcsn.org

Guiding Practitioners Toward Valuing and Implementing Family-Centered Practices
by S. L. McBride & M. J. Brotherson

Previously offered in *Reforming Personnel Preparation in Early Intervention*, this chapter, which highlights key concepts, methods, and materials, is now available online. The title says it all.

http://www.fpg.unc.edu/~scpp/pdfs/Reforming/10-253_276.pdf

Institute for Family-Centered Care

The Institute serves as a central resource for family members, administrators, policy makers, and members of the health care field, including medical education. This site shares information, facilitates problem solving, and promotes dialogue among individuals and organizations working toward family-centered care.

http://www.familycenteredcare.org/

Kids Together, Inc.

Get a family and consumer-eye view on family-based practices at this creative Web site. Cartoons, essays, links, and many other offerings can help practitioners see things from a different angle. Be sure to look at "When a Professional Says" (www.kidstogether.org/prof-say.htm), which is located in the "Perspectives" section.

http://www.kidstogether.org/

National Resource Center for Family-Centered Practices

The Center provides technical assistance, staff training, research and evaluation, and library research on family-based programs and issues to public and private human services agencies in states, counties, and communities across the United States. The Center has worked on child welfare, mental health, juvenile justice, community action, county extension, Head Start, and job training programs.

http://www.uiowa.edu/~nrcfcp/

Principles of Family-Centered Care ... (And How to Apply Them in Early Intervention!)

This thoughtful annotated list was produced by the Family Participation Task Group of the Massachusetts Early Intervention Interagency Coordinating Council in collaboration with the Massachusetts Department of Public Health.

http://www.spannj.org/Fall2001Bridge/family_centered_care.htm

DEC Recommended Practices

in Early Intervention/Early Childhood Special Education

Bridging the gap between research and practice, the book *DEC Recommended Practices* provides guidance on effective practices for working with young children with disabilities. The recommended practices are based on a review and synthesis of the research literature and the practices identified as critical by various stakeholders in early intervention/early childhood special education.

The book contains recommended practices in the following areas:

- Assessment—*John Neisworth and Stephen Bagnato*
- Child-focused interventions—*Mark Wolery*
- Family-based practices—*Carol Trivette and Carl Dunst*
- Interdisciplinary models—*R.A. McWilliam*
- Technology applications—*Kathleen Stremel*
- Policies, procedures, and systems change—*Gloria Harbin and Christine Salisbury*
- Personnel preparation—*Patricia Miller and Vicki Stayton*

In *DEC Recommended Practices*, you'll learn about the connection between early learning experiences and later school and work performance and how to bring those practices together to help educators, other practitioners, families, and administrators give children with disabilities quality learning experiences.

G143REC

SOPRIS WEST
EDUCATIONAL SERVICES

Phone: (800) 547-6747
Fax: (888) 819-7767
www.sopriswest.com

DEC Recommended Practices

Video: **Selected Strategies for Teaching Young Children With Special Needs**

This video demonstrates environments and several teaching procedures from *DEC Recommended Practices in Early Intervention/Early Childhood Special Education* (Sandall, McLean, & Smith, 2000), including:

- Peer-mediated strategies
- Using consequences
- Prompting strategies
- Naturalistic teaching procedures
- Environments that promote learning

These effective strategies are based on an extensive literature review and focus groups of parents, teachers, and administrators about what promotes learning for young children with special needs.

SOPRIS WEST EDUCATIONAL SERVICES

Phone: (800) 547-6747
Fax: (888) 819-7767
www.sopriswest.com

yOung Exceptional children

Monograph Series

The *Young Exceptional Children (YEC)* Monograph Series is designed for teachers, early care and education personnel, administrators, therapists, family members, and others who work with or on behalf of children, ages birth to eight, who have identified disabilities, developmental delays, are gifted/talented, or are at risk of future developmental delays or school difficulties.

One of the goals of the Series is to translate evidence-based findings into effective and useful strategies for practitioners and families. Articles in the *YEC* Monograph Series have a sound base in theory or research, yet are reader-friendly and written for a broad audience.

Monograph Series No. 1 – Practical Ideas for Addressing Challenging Behaviors

These articles offer proven interventions for challenging behaviors that can be used in early childhood programs and at home. Articles cover such topics as identification, prevention, environmental modifications, instruction of appropriate alternative behaviors, and more. *G143MONO1*

Monograph Series No. 2 – Natural Environments and Inclusion

With IDEA '97 prompting inclusive settings for children with disabilities, it is important to consider the natural settings in which these children are being taught and cared for—child care centers and preschools in particular. These articles include strategies for implementing effective individualized intervention within inclusive settings, ways to ensure that early childhood programs nurture positive attitudes and provide valuable experiences, and give examples of state and federal regulations that clarify changes in early intervention. *G143MONO2*

Monograph Series No. 3 – Teaching Strategies

The focus of this issue is on effective and doable teaching strategies that teachers can use in their early childhood classrooms or centers. Articles highlight teaching practices for a variety of curriculum content. *G143MONO3*

Monograph Series No. 4 – Assessment: Gathering Meaningful Information

Translating research findings into effective and useful assessment strategies is often a difficult and tedious task for practitioners and families. These articles provide practical ideas for conducting meaningful assessments of young children. Some of the topics addressed include:

- Linking assessment to intervention planning
- Involving families in the assessment process
- Evaluating the impact of culture and language on assessment
- Social, behavioral, and functional skills

G143MONO4

SOPRIS WEST
EDUCATIONAL SERVICES

Phone: (800) 547-6747
Fax: (888) 819-7767
www.sopriswest.com

Photocopy and send:
Division for Early Childhood
634 Eddy Avenue
Missoula, MT 59812-6696
(406) 243-5898
FAX (406) 243-4730

Annual Subscription
(four issues)

Individual	$20.00
Institutional	$35.00
International	$40.00 (U.S.)
Single Copy	$8.00

Prices subject to change without notice. Call to confirm.

☐ **Yes! I want to subscribe to**
Young Exceptional Children.

☐ Check/Money Order payable to DEC (U.S. dollars)
☐ Charge my credit card: ☐ VISA   ☐ MasterCard

Card Number _____ Exp. Date _____/_____

Signature _____

(No credit card orders can be shipped without signature and expiration date.)

Bill to _____   Ship to _____

Address _____   Address _____

_____   _____

Phone _____   Phone _____

Young Exceptional Children is **unique** *and* **practical**! *It is designed for any adult who works or lives with a young child who has a disability, developmental delay, special gifts or talents, or other special needs.*

Young Exceptional Children (YEC) is a peer-reviewed publication produced four times per year by the Division for Early Childhood (DEC) of the Council for Exceptional Children (CEC) with practical ideas for early childhood teachers, therapists, parents, and administrators. Topics include: challenging behaviors, family-guided routines, developmentally appropriate practices for children with special needs, best practices for young children with autism, strategies for successful inclusion, practical ideas for parents and professionals to promote learning and development, and more!